Walter Foster™

How to Draw

Disney's MULAN

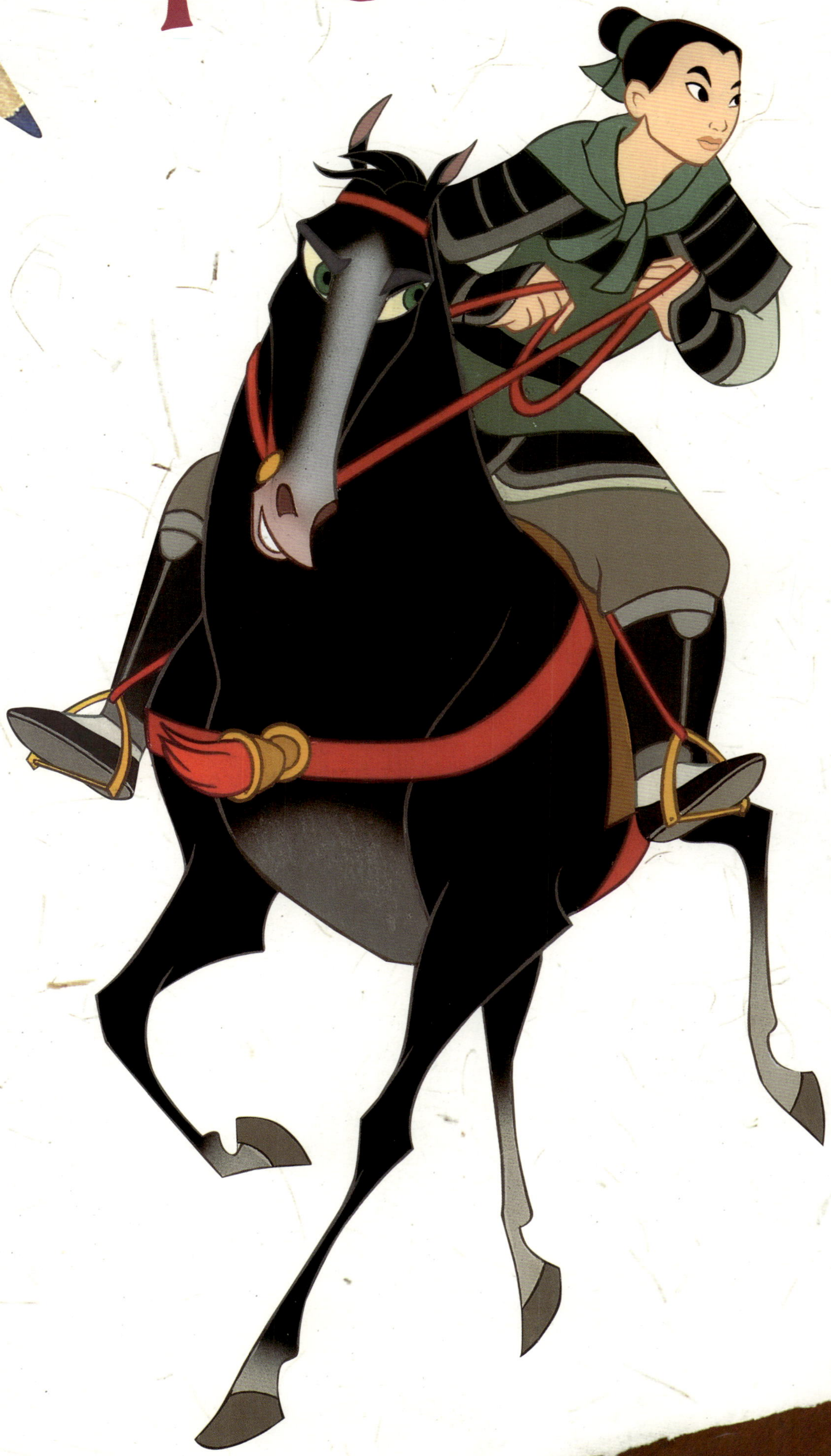

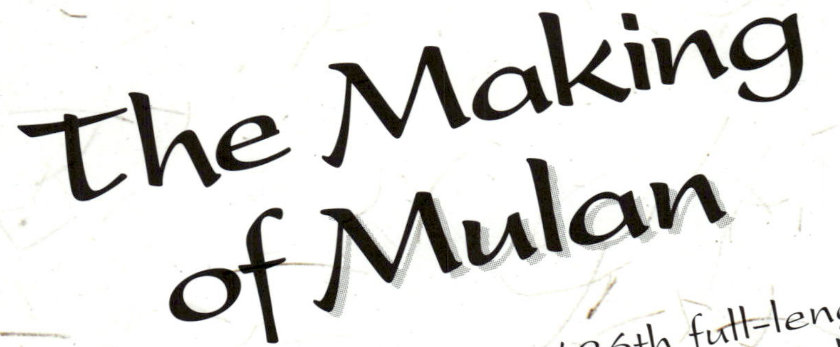

The Making of Mulan

In Walt Disney Pictures' 36th full-length animated feature film, a young woman named Mulan shows how great things can be accomplished through sheer determination, grace, and a great deal of heart. The same can be said of the animators who brought **Mulan** to life. To create the film, artists focused on graphically simple forms and smooth, flowing lines, echoing the graceful simplicity of Asian art. The story itself is based on a centuries-old Chinese legend.

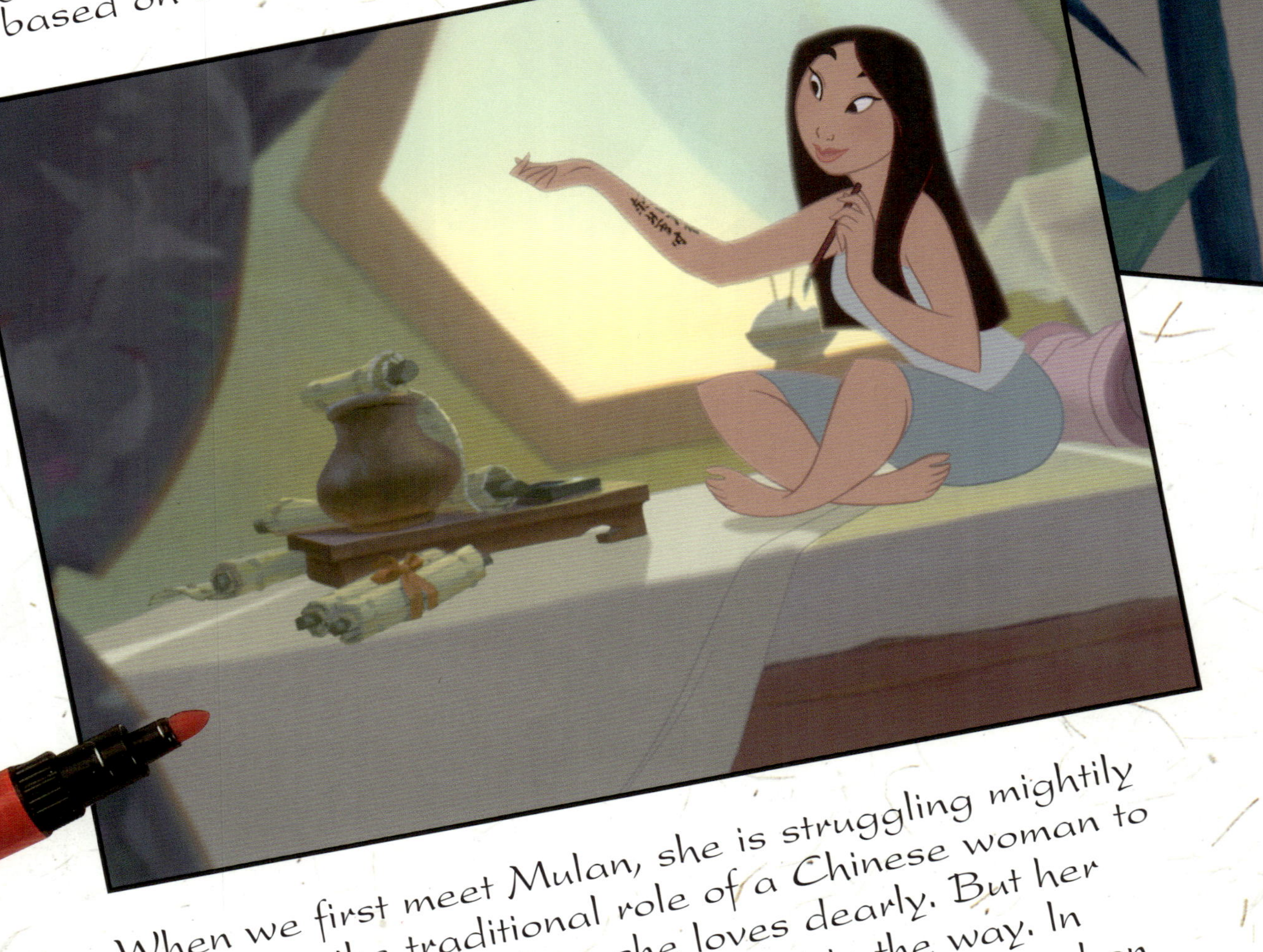

When we first meet Mulan, she is struggling mightily to assume the traditional role of a Chinese woman to please her father, whom she loves dearly. But her high spirits and bold approach get in the way. In designing Mulan's image, Disney artists focused on graceful, flowing shapes for her dark hair, her slightly angled eyes, and her athletic figure. Her feminine face is free of distracting details, yet her passionate spirit shines through.

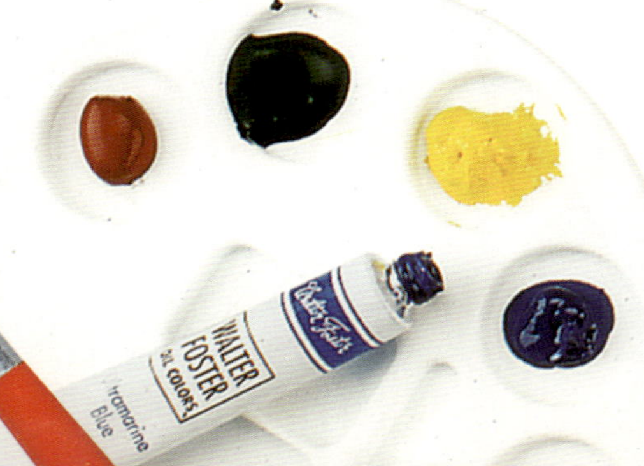

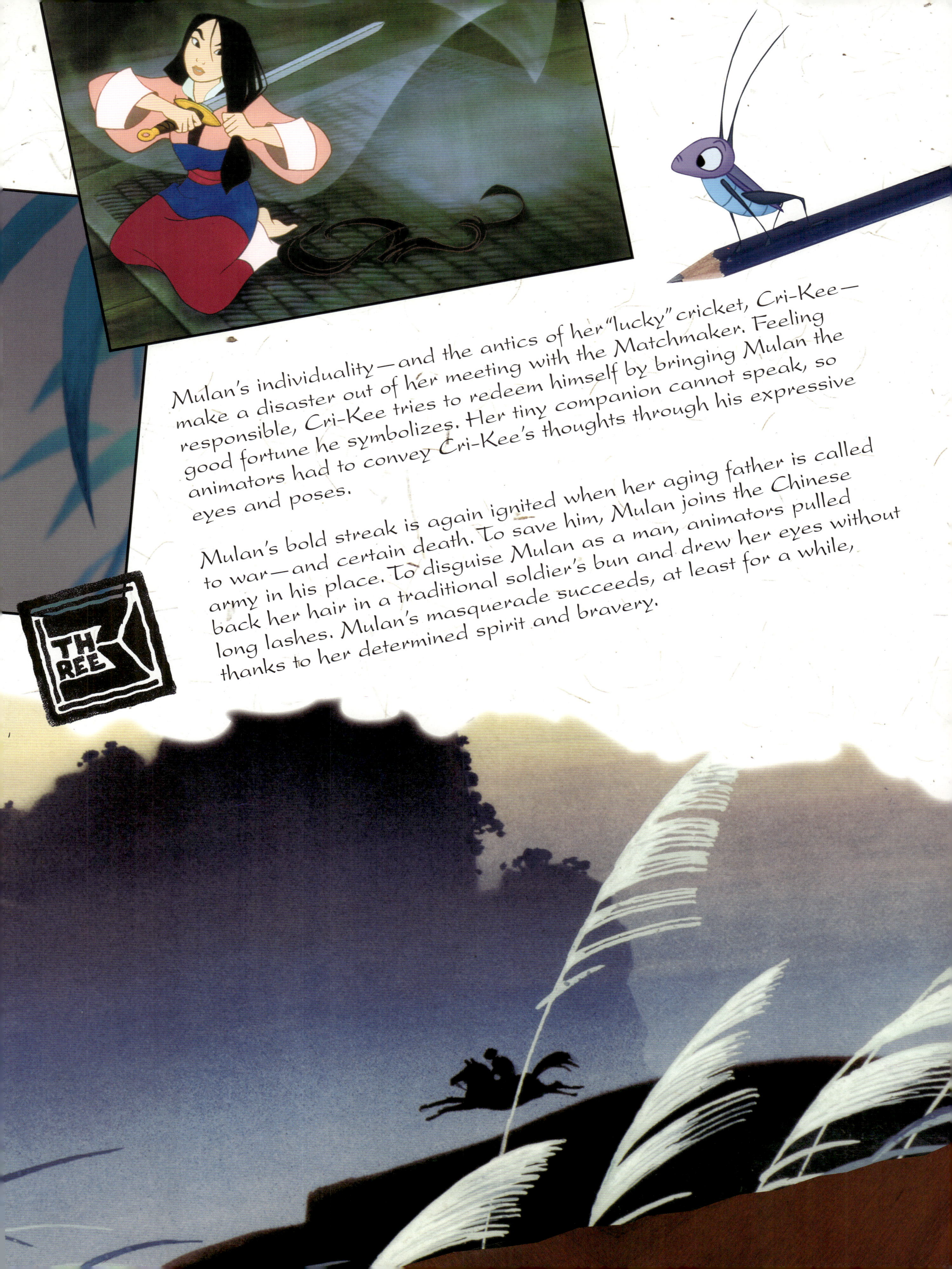

Mulan's individuality—and the antics of her "lucky" cricket, Cri-Kee—make a disaster out of her meeting with the Matchmaker. Feeling responsible, Cri-Kee tries to redeem himself by bringing Mulan the good fortune he symbolizes. Her tiny companion cannot speak, so animators had to convey Cri-Kee's thoughts through his expressive eyes and poses.

Mulan's bold streak is again ignited when her aging father is called to war—and certain death. To save him, Mulan joins the Chinese army in his place. To disguise Mulan as a man, animators pulled back her hair in a traditional soldier's bun and drew her eyes without long lashes. Mulan's masquerade succeeds, at least for a while, thanks to her determined spirit and bravery.

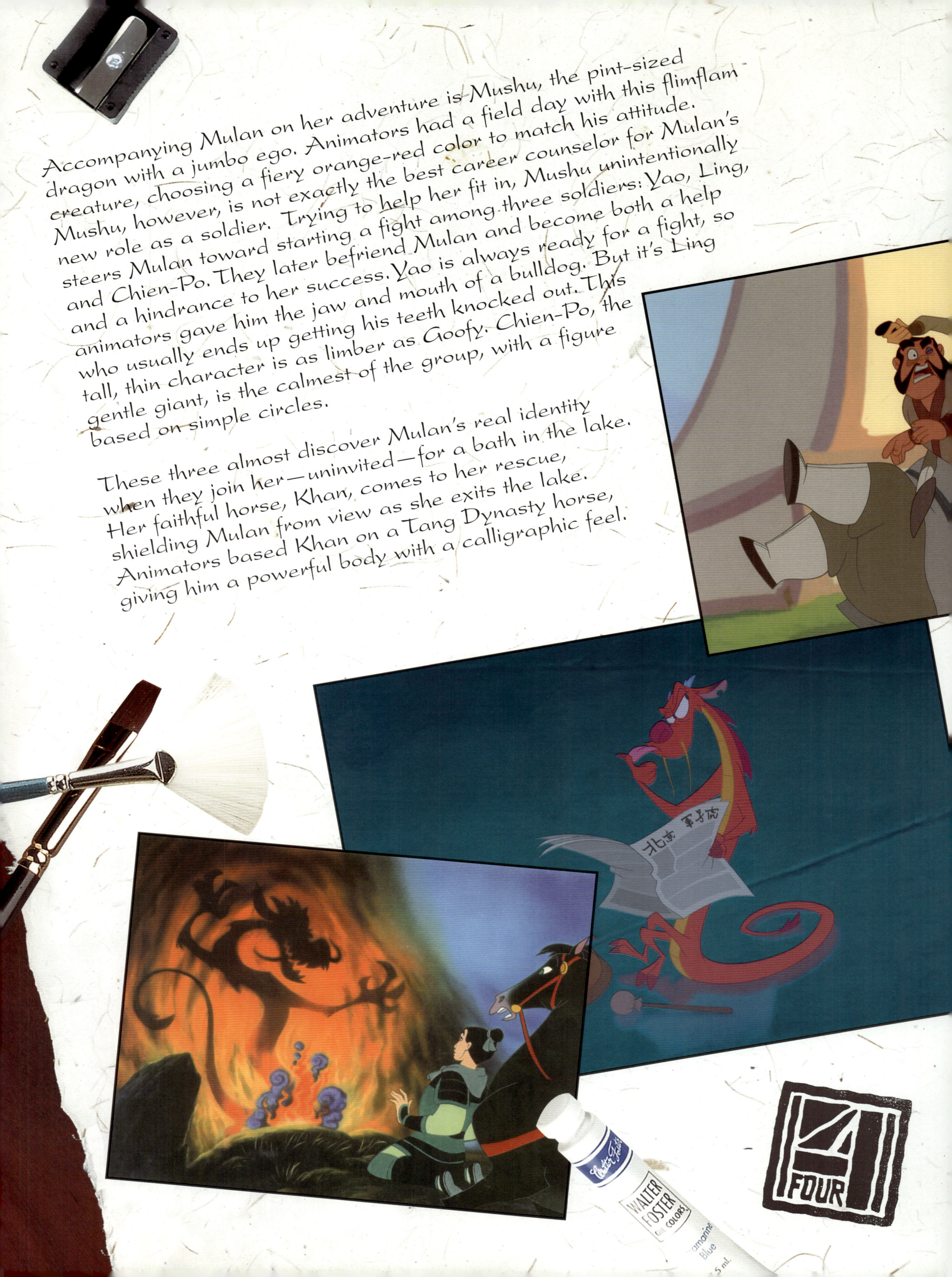

Accompanying Mulan on her adventure is Mushu, the pint-sized dragon with a jumbo ego. Animators had a field day with this flimflam creature, choosing a fiery orange-red color to match his attitude. Mushu, however, is not exactly the best career counselor for Mulan's new role as a soldier. Trying to help her fit in, Mushu unintentionally steers Mulan toward starting a fight among three soldiers: Yao, Ling, and Chien-Po. They later befriend Mulan and become both a help and a hindrance to her success. Yao is always ready for a fight, so animators gave him the jaw and mouth of a bulldog. But it's Ling who usually ends up getting his teeth knocked out. This tall, thin character is as limber as Goofy. Chien-Po, the gentle giant, is the calmest of the group, with a figure based on simple circles.

These three almost discover Mulan's real identity when they join her—uninvited—for a bath in the lake. Her faithful horse, Khan, comes to her rescue, shielding Mulan from view as she exits the lake. Animators based Khan on a Tang Dynasty horse, giving him a powerful body with a calligraphic feel.

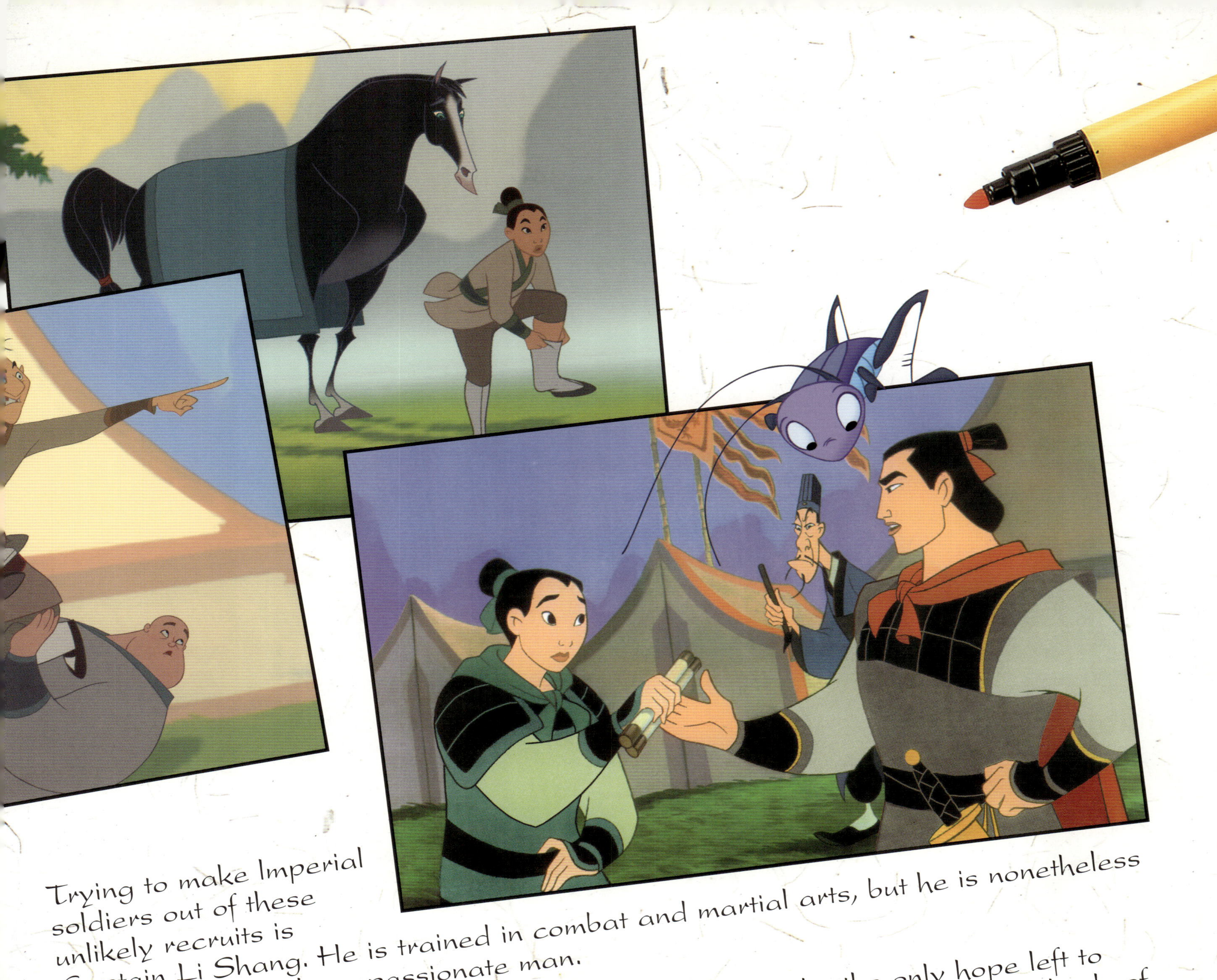

Trying to make Imperial soldiers out of these unlikely recruits is Captain Li Shang. He is trained in combat and martial arts, but he is nonetheless a considerate and compassionate man.

Shang's troops are sorely tested when they turn out to be the only hope left to defend the Emperor. They rise to battle the evil leader Shan-Yu and hundreds of Hun warriors. To show his great threat to China, Shan-Yu is drawn as a massive presence with larger-than-life proportions. He seems undefeatable, especially when compared to petite Mulan. Yet her quick thinking stops the entire Hun army when she causes an avalanche, which engulfs them in a sea of snow.

Unfortunately, Mulan's deception is discovered when she is wounded in battle. Because Shang feels betrayed by her, Mulan and her companions, Cri-Kee, Mushu, and Khan, are left behind when Shang moves his troops out. But when she discovers that the terrible Shan-Yu has survived and is proceeding toward the Imperial City, Mulan rises to the occasion yet again. Her ingenuity helps her defeat the Hun invaders once and for all. She saves the Emperor, earning Shang's respect and bringing honor to her beloved parents.

Now see if you can rise to the challenge of creating the characters from **Mulan.**

Equipment and Techniques

You will need only a few simple supplies to create the characters from **Mulan**. You may prefer working in graphite pencil to begin with, so you can erase any mistakes. Technical pens or pen and ink are other good drawing tools. You can also add color with felt-tip markers, colored pencils, watercolor, or acrylic paint. The choice is yours!

In this book, you'll be shown how to draw the characters from **Mulan** in a few simple steps. You will also get helpful tips and useful information from Disney artists to guide you through the process of drawing. You'll be amazed at how easy it is to make your own works of art.

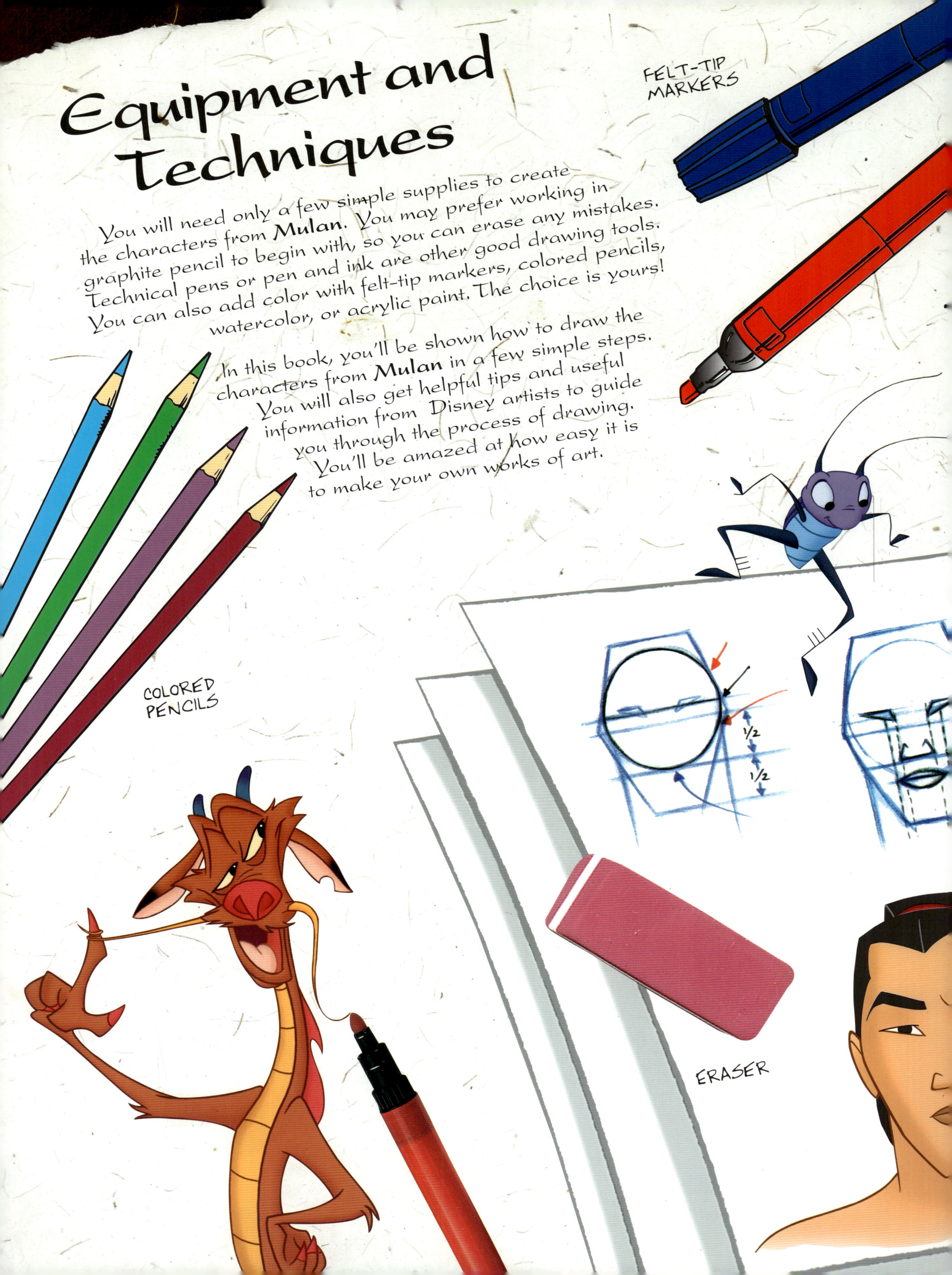

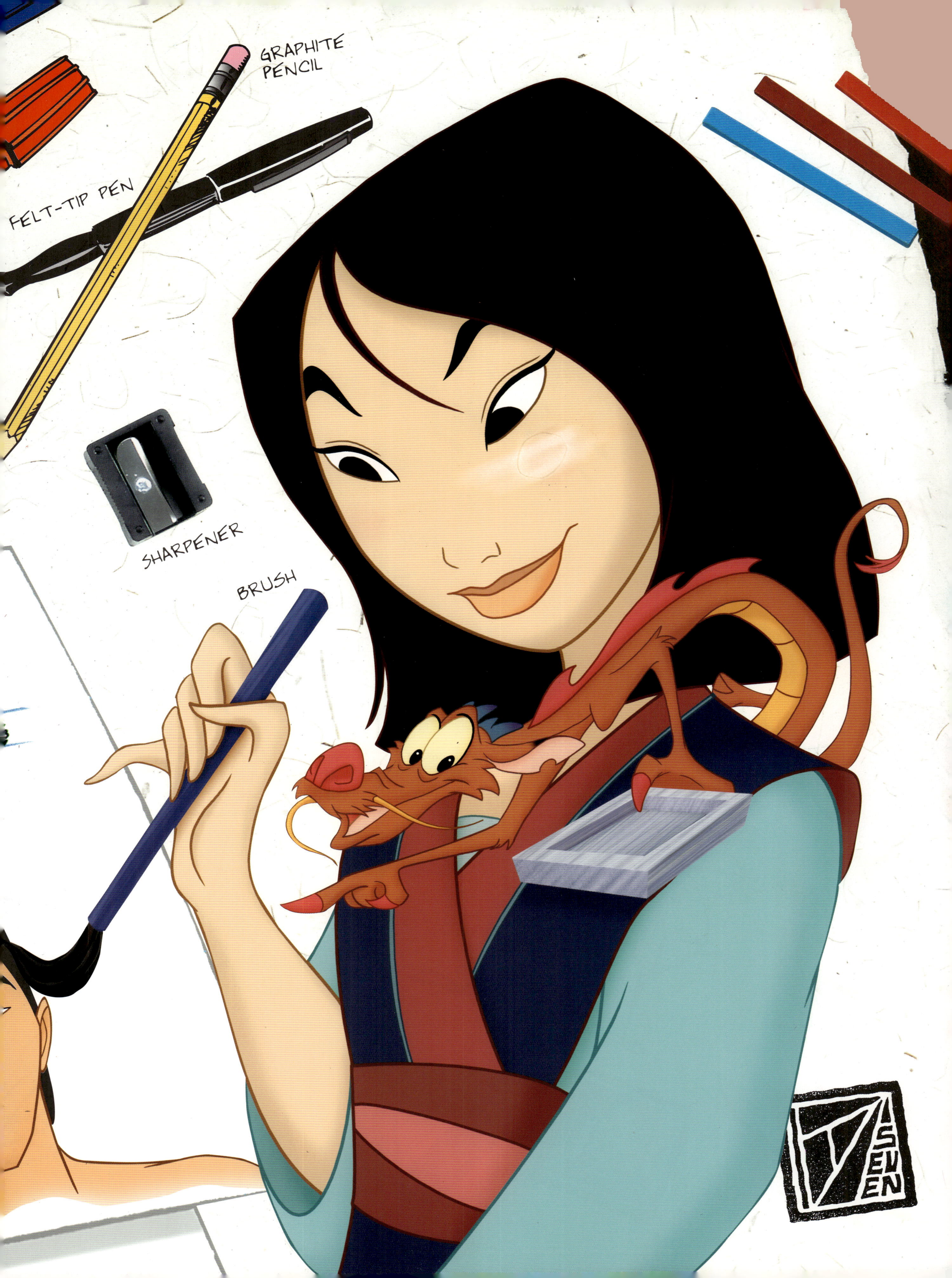
GRAPHITE PENCIL
FELT-TIP PEN
SHARPENER
BRUSH

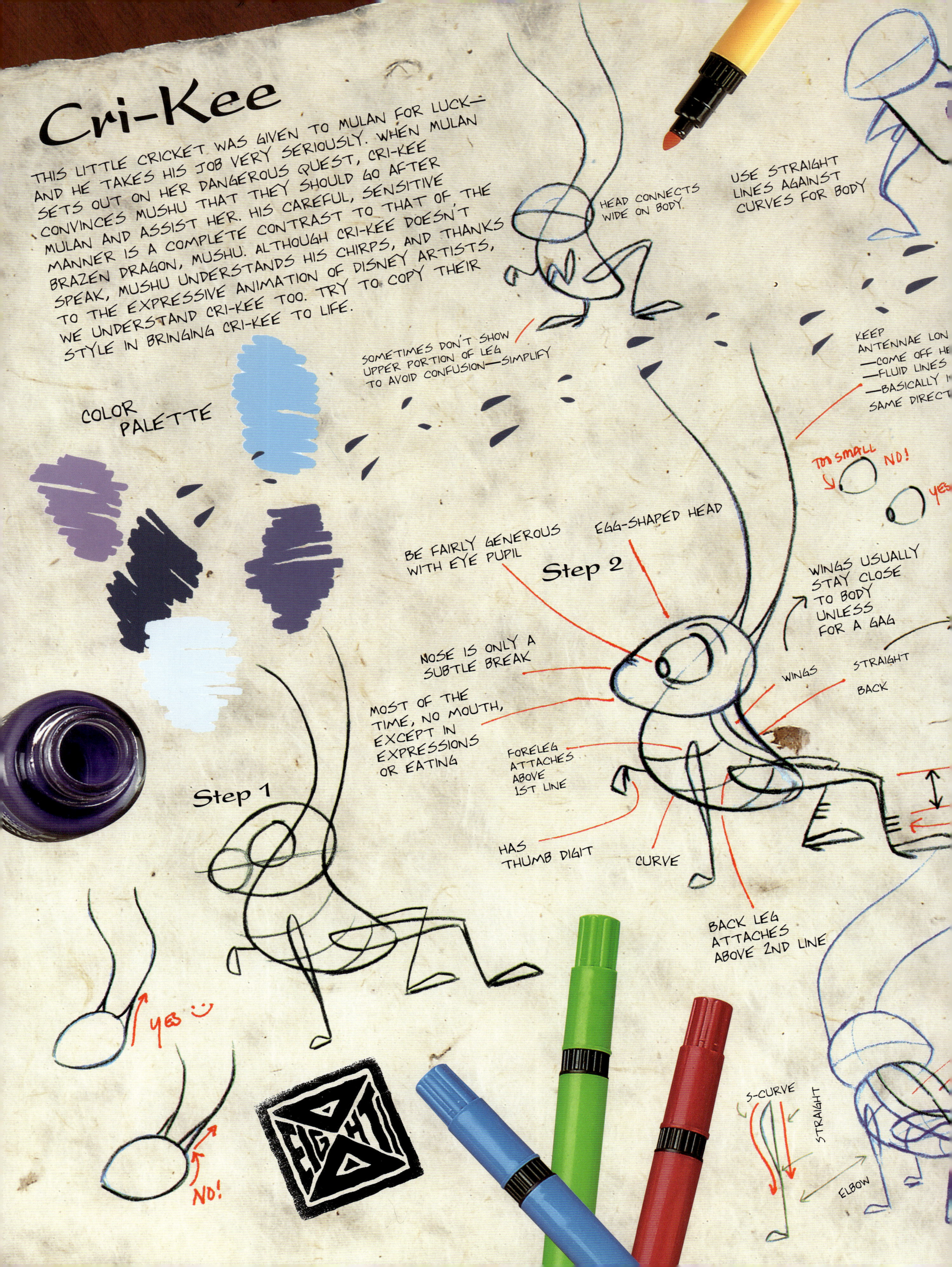

Cri-Kee
THIS LITTLE CRICKET WAS GIVEN TO MULAN FOR LUCK—AND HE TAKES HIS JOB VERY SERIOUSLY. WHEN MULAN SETS OUT ON HER DANGEROUS QUEST, CRI-KEE CONVINCES MUSHU THAT THEY SHOULD GO AFTER MULAN AND ASSIST HER. HIS CAREFUL, SENSITIVE MANNER IS A COMPLETE CONTRAST TO THAT OF THE BRAZEN DRAGON, MUSHU. ALTHOUGH CRI-KEE DOESN'T SPEAK, MUSHU UNDERSTANDS HIS CHIRPS, AND THANKS TO THE EXPRESSIVE ANIMATION OF DISNEY ARTISTS, WE UNDERSTAND CRI-KEE TOO. TRY TO COPY THEIR STYLE IN BRINGING CRI-KEE TO LIFE.
COLOR PALETTE
HEAD CONNECTS WIDE ON BODY
USE STRAIGHT LINES AGAINST CURVES FOR BODY
SOMETIMES DON'T SHOW UPPER PORTION OF LEG TO AVOID CONFUSION—SIMPLIFY
KEEP
ANTENNAE
—COME OFF
—FLUID LINES
—BASICALLY
SAME
TOO SMALL
NO!
EGG-SHAPED HEAD
BE FAIRLY GENEROUS WITH EYE PUPIL
Step 2
WINGS USUALLY STAY CLOSE TO BODY UNLESS FOR A GAG
NOSE IS ONLY A SUBTLE BREAK
WINGS
STRAIGHT
BACK
MOST OF THE TIME, NO MOUTH, EXCEPT IN EXPRESSIONS OR EATING
FORELEG ATTACHES ABOVE 1ST LINE
Step 1
HAS THUMB DIGIT
CURVE
BACK LEG ATTACHES ABOVE 2ND LINE
YES
NO!
S-CURVE
STRAIGHT
ELBOW

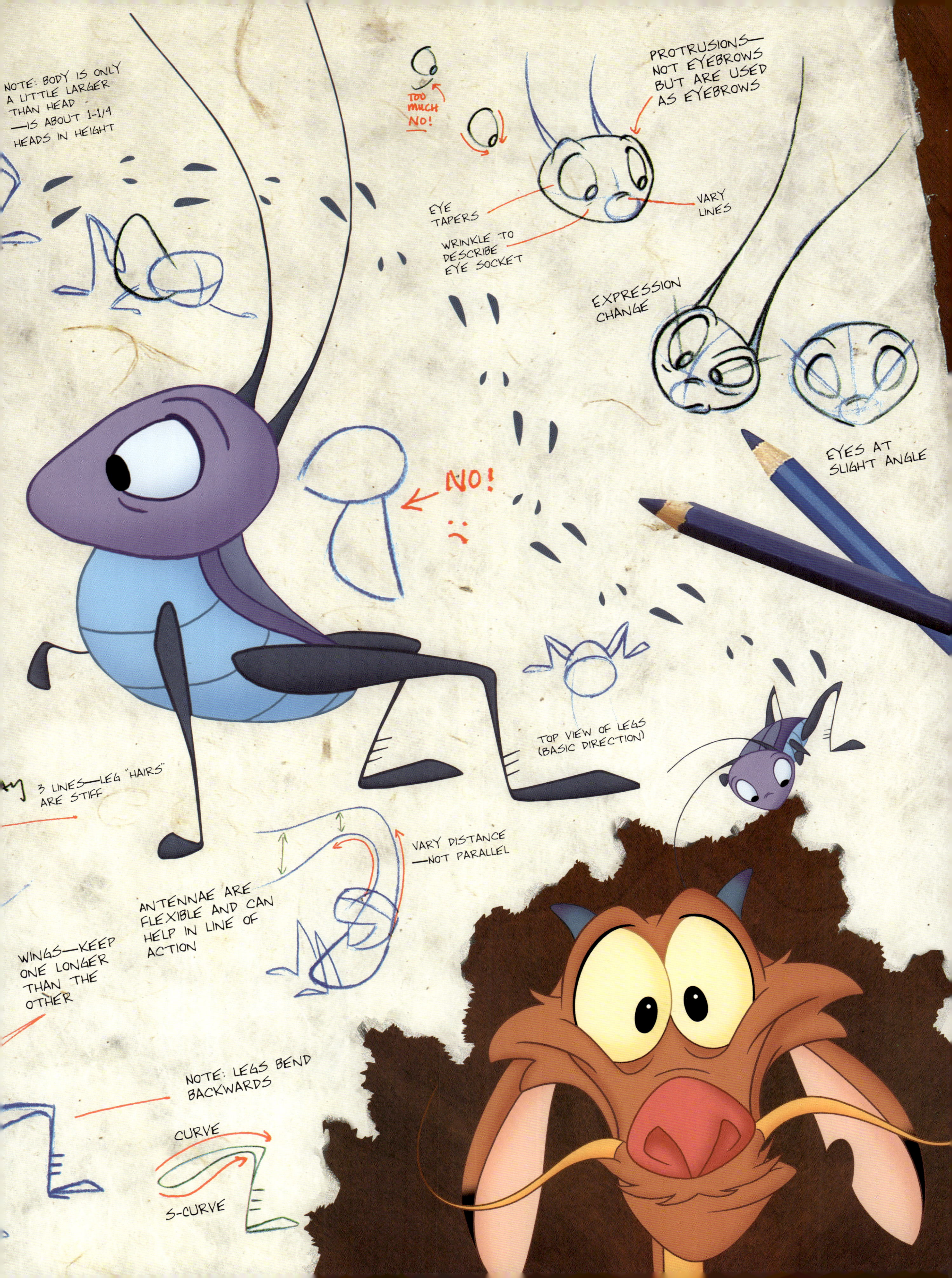

NOTE: BODY IS ONLY A LITTLE LARGER THAN HEAD —IS ABOUT 1-1/4 HEADS IN HEIGHT
TOO MUCH NO!
PROTRUSIONS— NOT EYEBROWS BUT ARE USED AS EYEBROWS
EYE TAPERS
VARY LINES
WRINKLE TO DESCRIBE EYE SOCKET
EXPRESSION CHANGE
EYES AT SLIGHT ANGLE
NO!
TOP VIEW OF LEGS (BASIC DIRECTION)
3 LINES—LEG "HAIRS" ARE STIFF
VARY DISTANCE —NOT PARALLEL
ANTENNAE ARE FLEXIBLE AND CAN HELP IN LINE OF ACTION
WINGS—KEEP ONE LONGER THAN THE OTHER
NOTE: LEGS BEND BACKWARDS
CURVE
S-CURVE

Mushu

MUSHU HAS A BIG MOUTH FOR A LITTLE GUY—FIGURATIVELY SPEAKING, THAT IS. HIS BIG-SHOT TALK GOT HIM INTO TROUBLE WITH MULAN'S FAMILY ANCESTORS. NOW HE'S DETERMINED TO HELP MULAN, ALTHOUGH HE'S ONLY AS TALL AS HER KNEE. BUT YOU CAN DRAW HIM ON A LARGER SCALE TO SHOW OFF HIS CATFISH WHISKERS AND COW EARS. NOTE THAT HIS SNAKELIKE BODY FLOWS CONTINUOUSLY FROM THE TIP OF HIS TAIL TO HIS MOUTH.

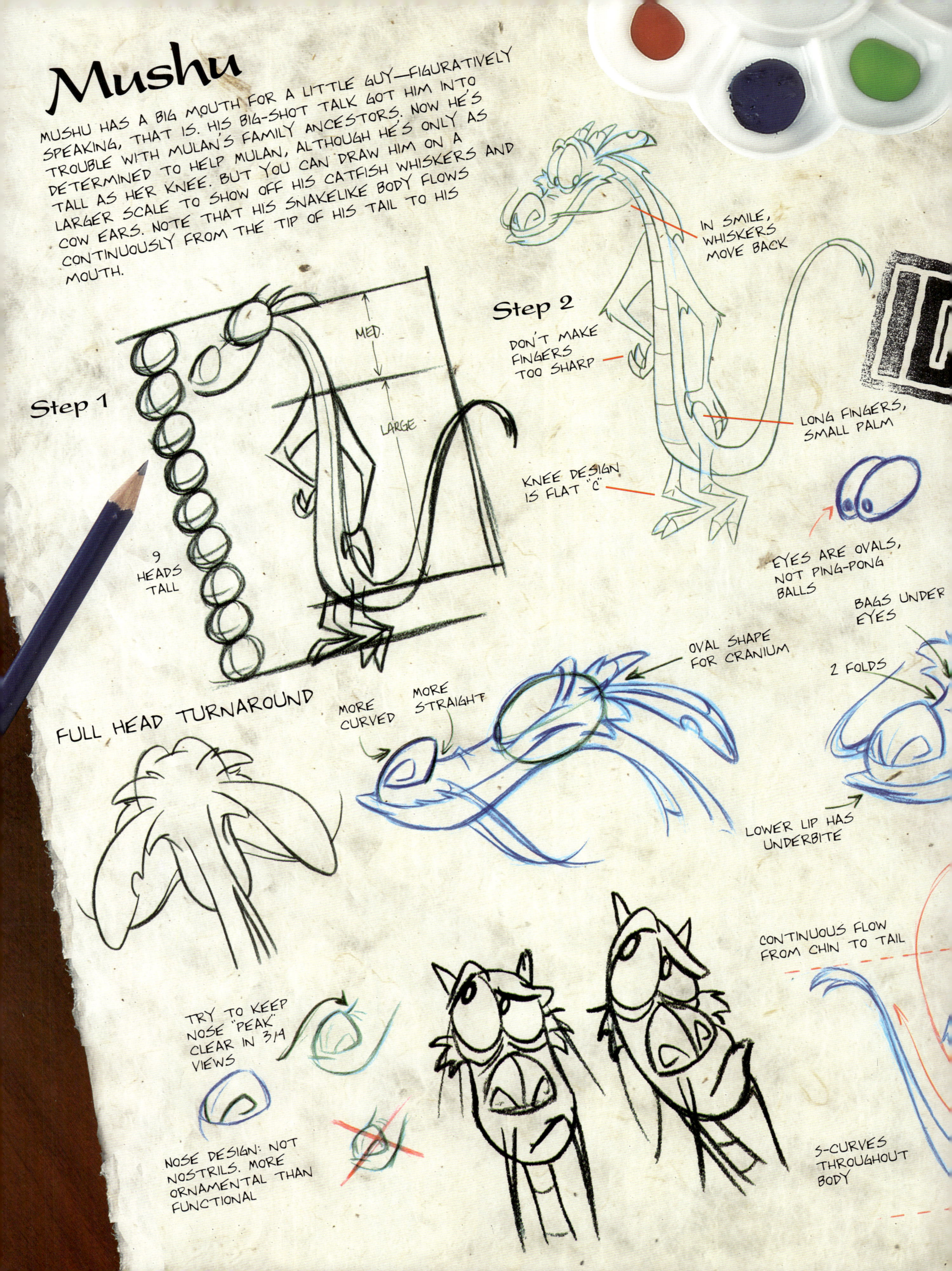

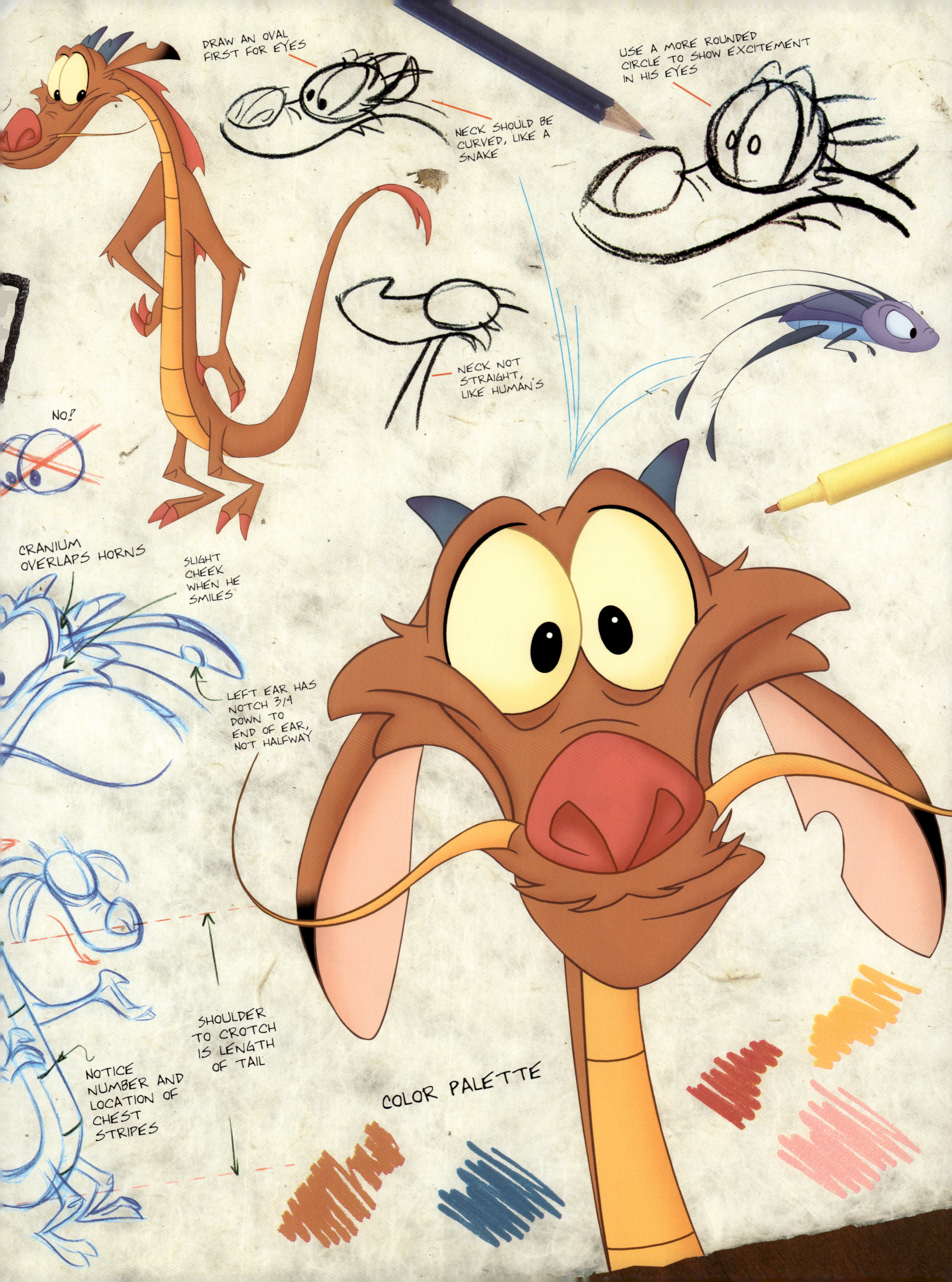
DRAW AN OVAL FIRST FOR EYES
USE A MORE ROUNDED CIRCLE TO SHOW EXCITEMENT IN HIS EYES
NECK SHOULD BE CURVED, LIKE A SNAKE
NECK NOT STRAIGHT, LIKE HUMAN'S
NO!
CRANIUM OVERLAPS HORNS
SLIGHT CHEEK WHEN HE SMILES
LEFT EAR HAS NOTCH 3/4 DOWN TO END OF EAR, NOT HALFWAY
SHOULDER TO CROTCH IS LENGTH OF TAIL
NOTICE NUMBER AND LOCATION OF CHEST STRIPES
COLOR PALETTE

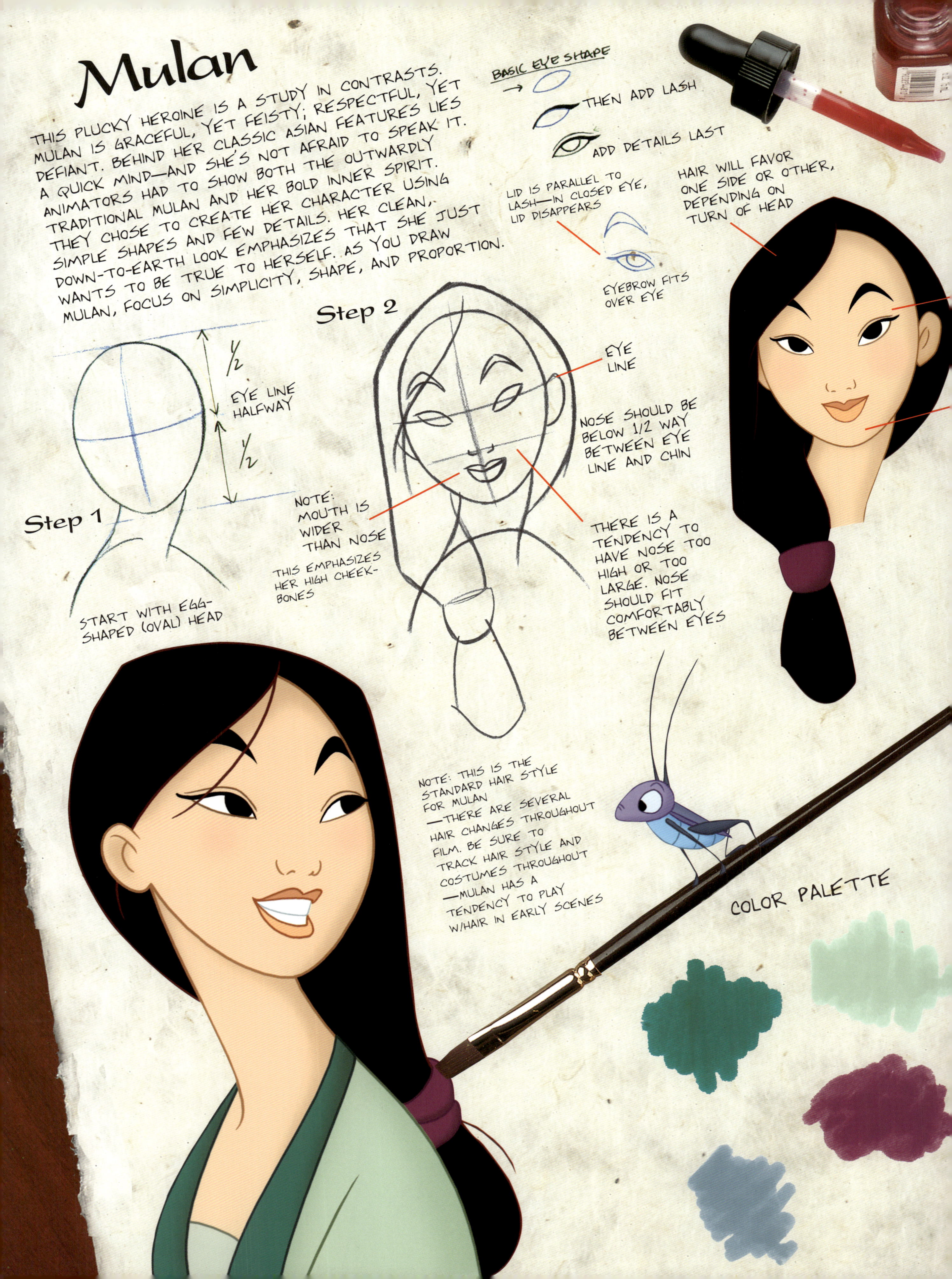
Mulan
THIS PLUCKY HEROINE IS A STUDY IN CONTRASTS. MULAN IS GRACEFUL, YET FEISTY; RESPECTFUL, YET DEFIANT. BEHIND HER CLASSIC ASIAN FEATURES LIES A QUICK MIND—AND SHE'S NOT AFRAID TO SPEAK IT. ANIMATORS HAD TO SHOW BOTH THE OUTWARDLY TRADITIONAL MULAN AND HER BOLD INNER SPIRIT. THEY CHOSE TO CREATE HER CHARACTER USING SIMPLE SHAPES AND FEW DETAILS. HER CLEAN, DOWN-TO-EARTH LOOK EMPHASIZES THAT SHE JUST WANTS TO BE TRUE TO HERSELF. AS YOU DRAW MULAN, FOCUS ON SIMPLICITY, SHAPE, AND PROPORTION.
BASIC EYE SHAPE
THEN ADD LASH
ADD DETAILS LAST
LID IS PARALLEL TO LASH—IN CLOSED EYE, LID DISAPPEARS
EYEBROW FITS OVER EYE
HAIR WILL FAVOR ONE SIDE OR OTHER, DEPENDING ON TURN OF HEAD
Step 1
1/2
EYE LINE HALFWAY
1/2
START WITH EGG-SHAPED (OVAL) HEAD
Step 2
EYE LINE
NOSE SHOULD BE BELOW 1/2 WAY BETWEEN EYE LINE AND CHIN
NOTE: MOUTH IS WIDER THAN NOSE
THIS EMPHASIZES HER HIGH CHEEK-BONES
THERE IS A TENDENCY TO HAVE NOSE TOO HIGH OR TOO LARGE. NOSE SHOULD FIT COMFORTABLY BETWEEN EYES
NOTE: THIS IS THE STANDARD HAIR STYLE FOR MULAN —THERE ARE SEVERAL HAIR CHANGES THROUGHOUT FILM. BE SURE TO TRACK HAIR STYLE AND COSTUMES THROUGHOUT —MULAN HAS A TENDENCY TO PLAY W/HAIR IN EARLY SCENES
COLOR PALETTE

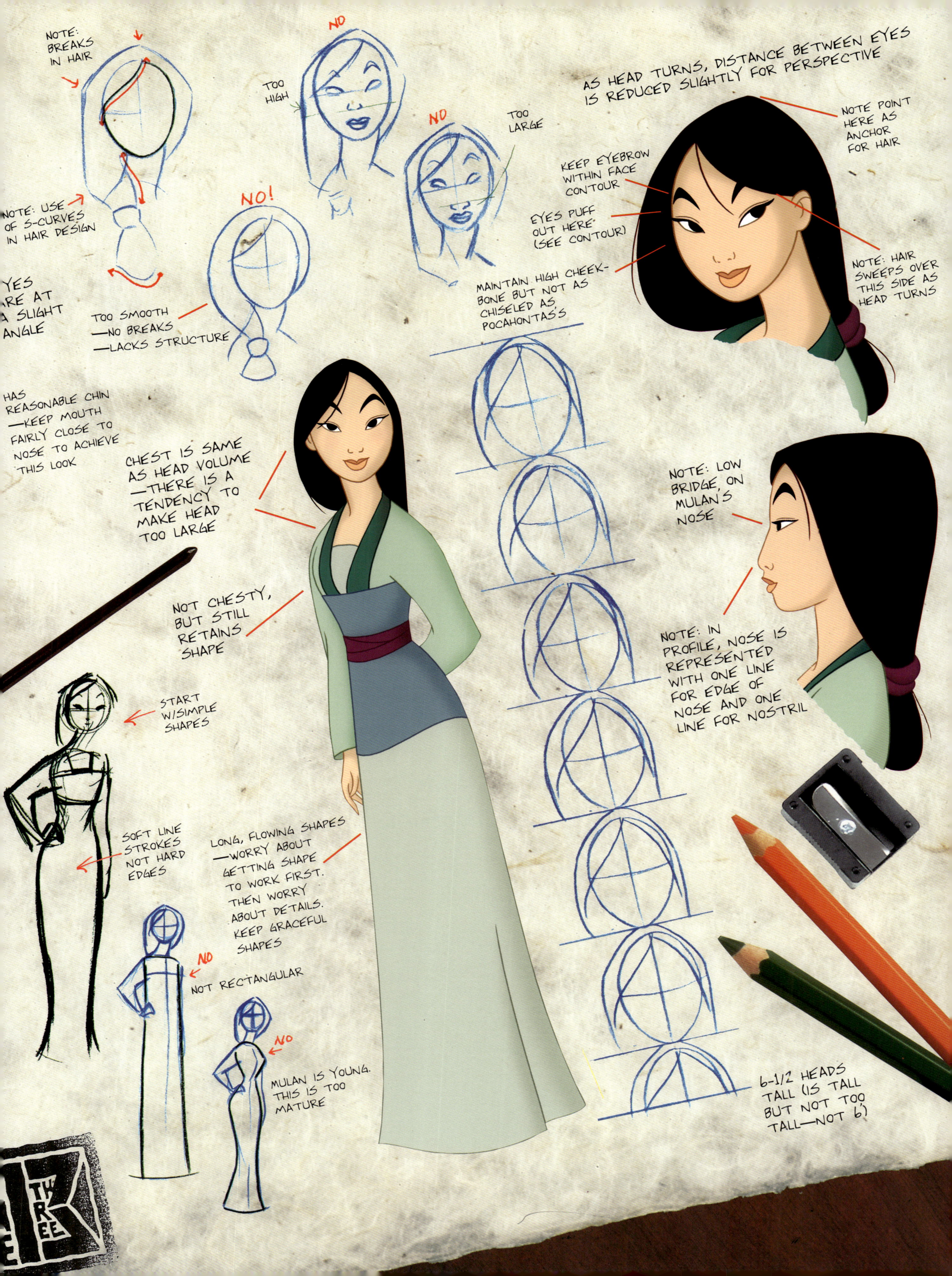
NOTE: BREAKS IN HAIR
NOTE: USE OF S-CURVES IN HAIR DESIGN
NO
TOO HIGH
NO
TOO LARGE
NO!
TOO SMOOTH —NO BREAKS —LACKS STRUCTURE
AS HEAD TURNS, DISTANCE BETWEEN EYES IS REDUCED SLIGHTLY FOR PERSPECTIVE
NOTE POINT HERE AS ANCHOR FOR HAIR
KEEP EYEBROW WITHIN FACE CONTOUR
EYES PUFF OUT HERE (SEE CONTOUR)
MAINTAIN HIGH CHEEK-BONE BUT NOT AS CHISELED AS POCAHONTAS'S
NOTE: HAIR SWEEPS OVER THIS SIDE AS HEAD TURNS
HAS REASONABLE CHIN —KEEP MOUTH FAIRLY CLOSE TO NOSE TO ACHIEVE THIS LOOK
CHEST IS SAME AS HEAD VOLUME —THERE IS A TENDENCY TO MAKE HEAD TOO LARGE
NOTE: LOW BRIDGE, ON MULAN'S NOSE
NOT CHESTY, BUT STILL RETAINS SHAPE
NOTE: IN PROFILE, NOSE IS REPRESENTED WITH ONE LINE FOR EDGE OF NOSE AND ONE LINE FOR NOSTRIL
START W/SIMPLE SHAPES
SOFT LINE STROKES NOT HARD EDGES
LONG, FLOWING SHAPES —WORRY ABOUT GETTING SHAPE TO WORK FIRST. THEN WORRY ABOUT DETAILS. KEEP GRACEFUL SHAPES
NO
NOT RECTANGULAR
NO
MULAN IS YOUNG. THIS IS TOO MATURE
6-1/2 HEADS TALL (IS TALL BUT NOT TOO TALL—NOT 6')

Mulan as Soldier

MULAN BECOMES A SOLDIER TO SAVE HER ELDERLY FATHER'S LIFE. SHE DEFIES TRADITION, DOING WHAT SHE BELIEVES IS RIGHT. THE FILM'S ARTISTS HAVE FOLLOWED HER DARING LEAD AND TREATED HER "SOLDIER" LOOK WITH AN UNCONVENTIONAL APPROACH. HER BASIC FEATURES ARE THE SAME, BUT SLIGHT CHANGES HAVE BEEN MADE TO HELP HIDE HER FEMININITY. HERE ARE SOME SECRETS TO DRAWING MULAN AS A SOLDIER:

ON FRONT VIEW, HAIR BUN IS A "CHEAT" LIKE MICKEY'S EARS —IS RAISED SLIGHTLY FOR A BETTER SILHOUETTE

WIDOW'S PEAK

NOTE: TAPERS UP—HAIR IS CLOSER TO HEAD (PULLED BACK)

NOTE: SLIGHT S-CURVE

SLIGHTLY SMALLER EYES —NOTICE EYE HAS NO "TAIL" LASH OR LID INDICATION LIKE "NORMAL" MULAN EYES

MULAN'S FATHER'S SWORD WHICH SHE TAKES WITH HER TO THE ARMY

EARS STICK OUT PROMINENTLY

SLIGHTLY ANGLED-OUT JAWLINE

NOT PENCIL NECK (IS ATHLETIC) BUT NOT LINEBACKER NECK

LIPS ARE SLIGHTLY LESS CURVY THAN ON "NORMAL" MULAN AND ARE NATURAL IN COLOR —SLIGHTLY THINNER

DO NOT DRAW HER LIPS LIKE THOSE OF MEN

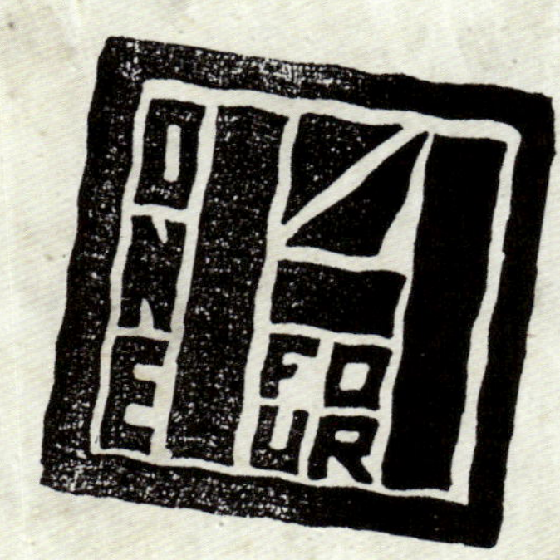

Step 1

—MAP OUT POSE FIRST, THEN COMPENSATE ARMOR TO FIT

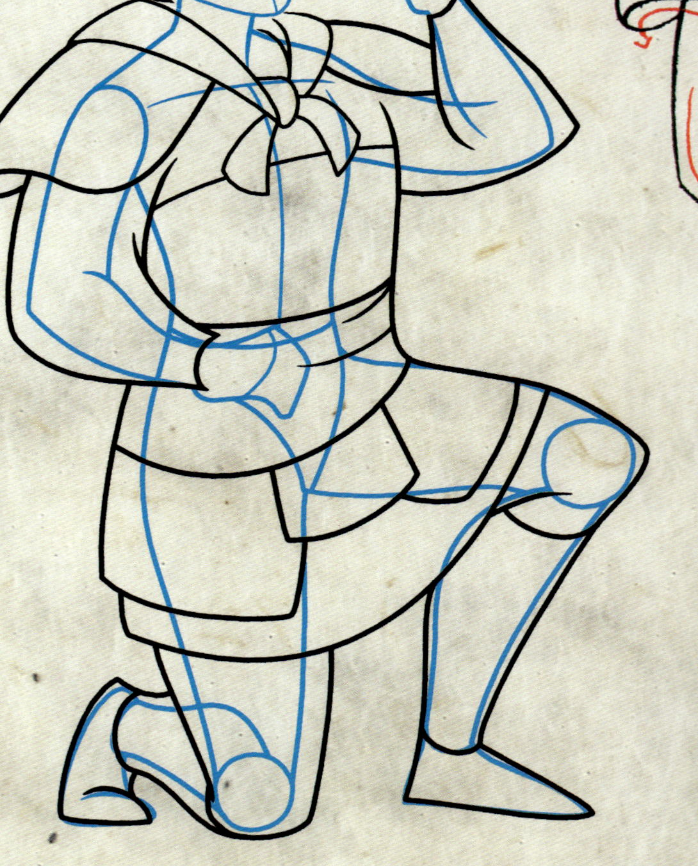

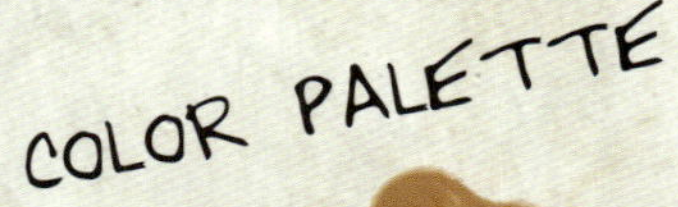

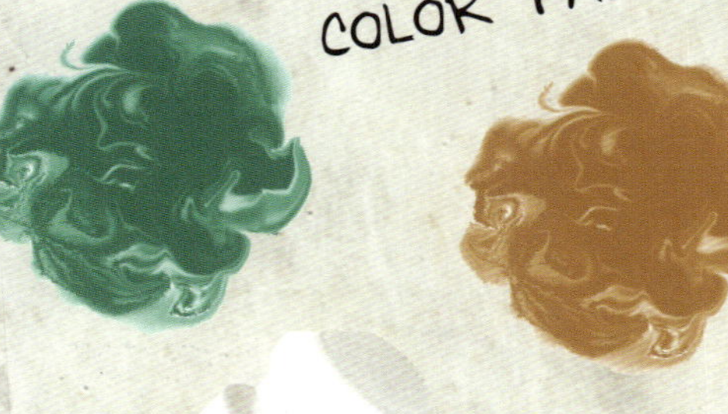

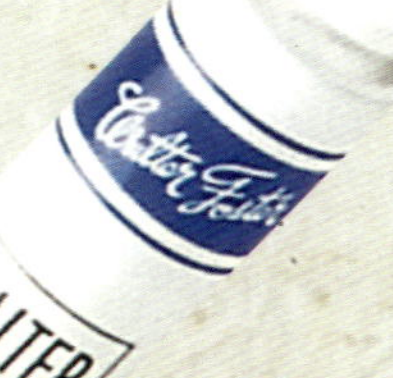

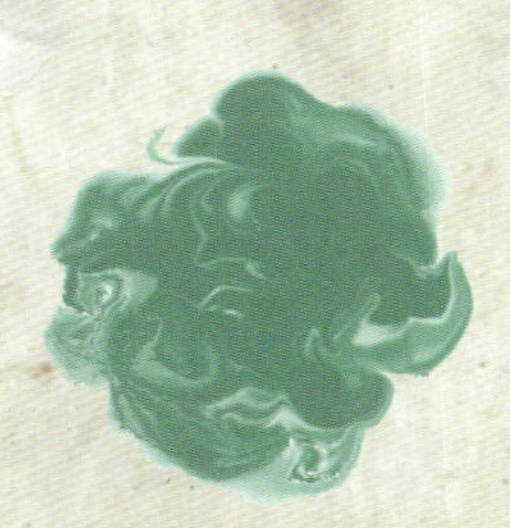

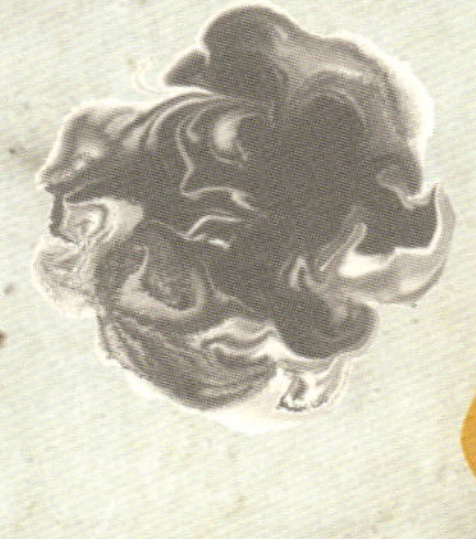

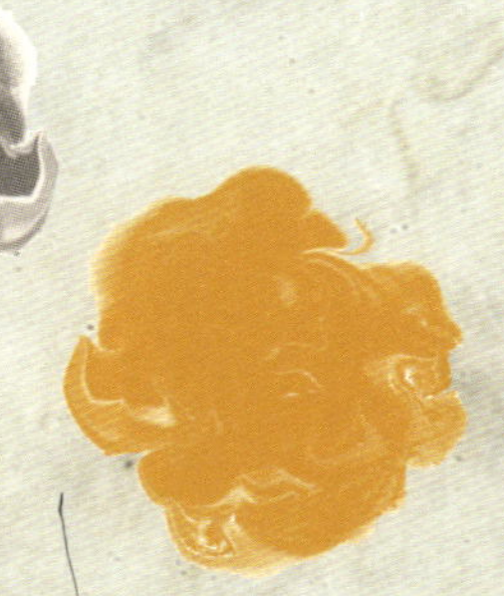

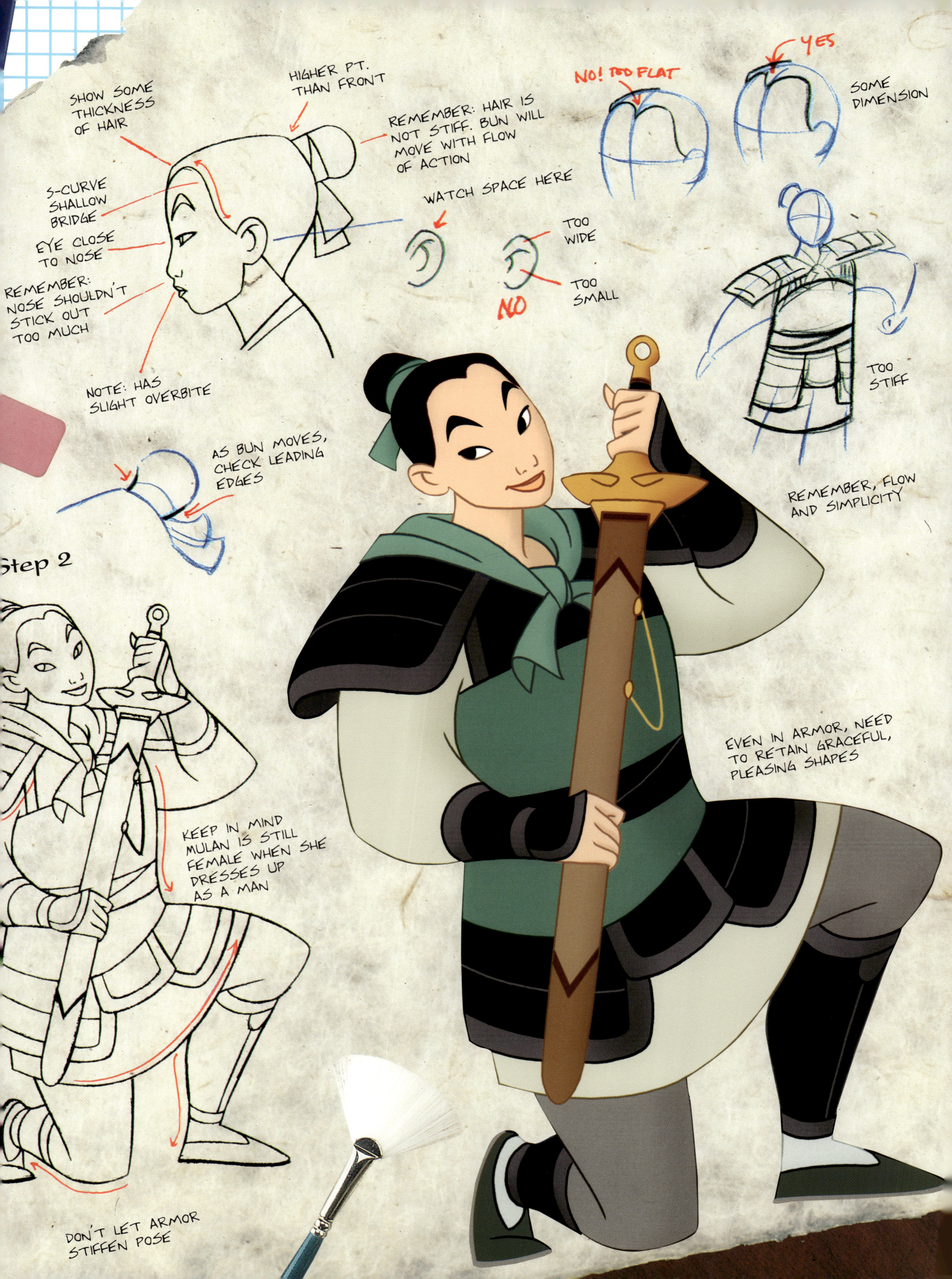
SHOW SOME THICKNESS OF HAIR
HIGHER PT. THAN FRONT
REMEMBER: HAIR IS NOT STIFF. BUN WILL MOVE WITH FLOW OF ACTION
NO! TOO FLAT
YES
SOME DIMENSION
S-CURVE SHALLOW BRIDGE
EYE CLOSE TO NOSE
REMEMBER: NOSE SHOULDN'T STICK OUT TOO MUCH
WATCH SPACE HERE
TOO WIDE
TOO SMALL
NO
NOTE: HAS SLIGHT OVERBITE
TOO STIFF
AS BUN MOVES, CHECK LEADING EDGES
REMEMBER, FLOW AND SIMPLICITY
Step 2
EVEN IN ARMOR, NEED TO RETAIN GRACEFUL, PLEASING SHAPES
KEEP IN MIND MULAN IS STILL FEMALE WHEN SHE DRESSES UP AS A MAN
DON'T LET ARMOR STIFFEN POSE

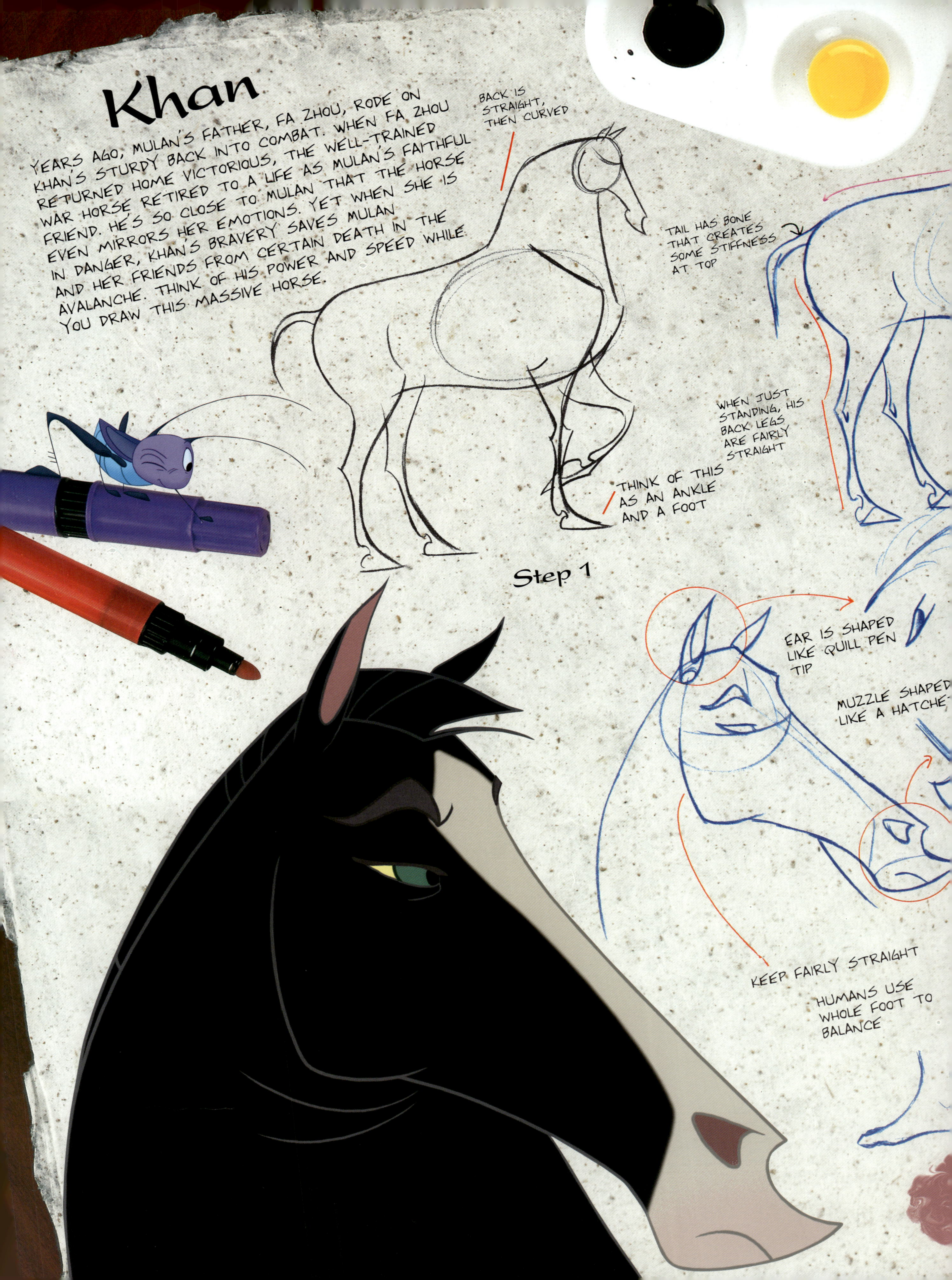

Khan

YEARS AGO, MULAN'S FATHER, FA ZHOU, RODE ON KHAN'S STURDY BACK INTO COMBAT. WHEN FA ZHOU RETURNED HOME VICTORIOUS, THE WELL-TRAINED WAR HORSE RETIRED TO A LIFE AS MULAN'S FAITHFUL FRIEND. HE'S SO CLOSE TO MULAN THAT THE HORSE EVEN MIRRORS HER EMOTIONS. YET WHEN SHE IS IN DANGER, KHAN'S BRAVERY SAVES MULAN AND HER FRIENDS FROM CERTAIN DEATH IN THE AVALANCHE. THINK OF HIS POWER AND SPEED WHILE YOU DRAW THIS MASSIVE HORSE.

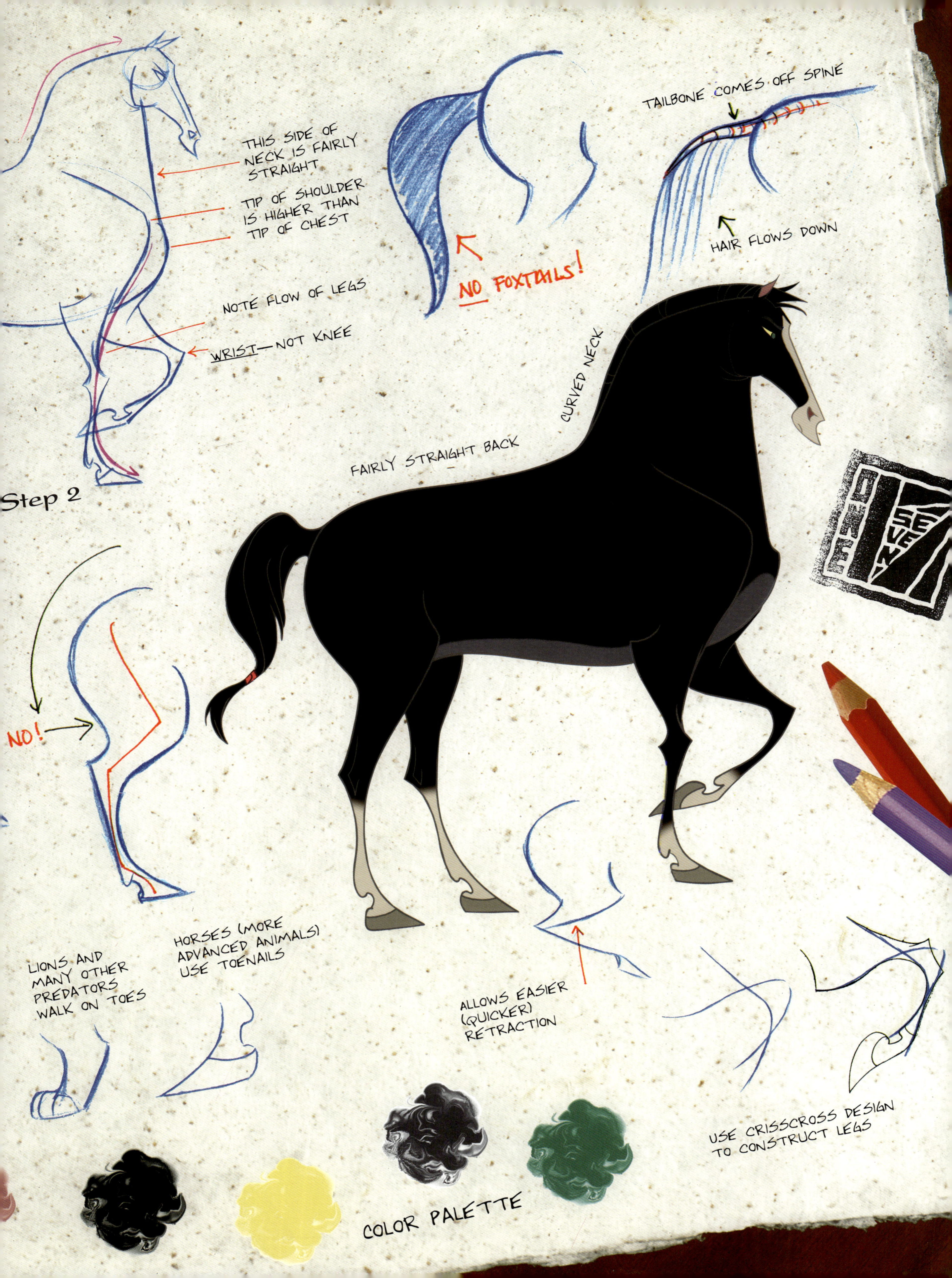
THIS SIDE OF NECK IS FAIRLY STRAIGHT
TIP OF SHOULDER IS HIGHER THAN TIP OF CHEST
NOTE FLOW OF LEGS
WRIST—NOT KNEE
NO FOXTAILS!
TAILBONE COMES OFF SPINE
HAIR FLOWS DOWN
CURVED NECK
FAIRLY STRAIGHT BACK
Step 2
NO!
LIONS AND MANY OTHER PREDATORS WALK ON TOES
HORSES (MORE ADVANCED ANIMALS) USE TOENAILS
ALLOWS EASIER (QUICKER) RETRACTION
USE CRISSCROSS DESIGN TO CONSTRUCT LEGS
COLOR PALETTE

Khan in Action

MULAN'S HORSE SHOWS SURPRISING GRACE AND AGILITY FOR SUCH A STRONG ANIMAL. KHAN HAD TO RACE THROUGH SWIRLING SNOW TO SAVE MULAN FROM THE ADVANCING AVALANCHE. DRAW KHAN RUNNING GRACEFULLY ON HIS POINTED HOOVES, BUT KEEP HIS CHEST LARGE AND ROUND TO SIGNIFY HIS STRENGTH.

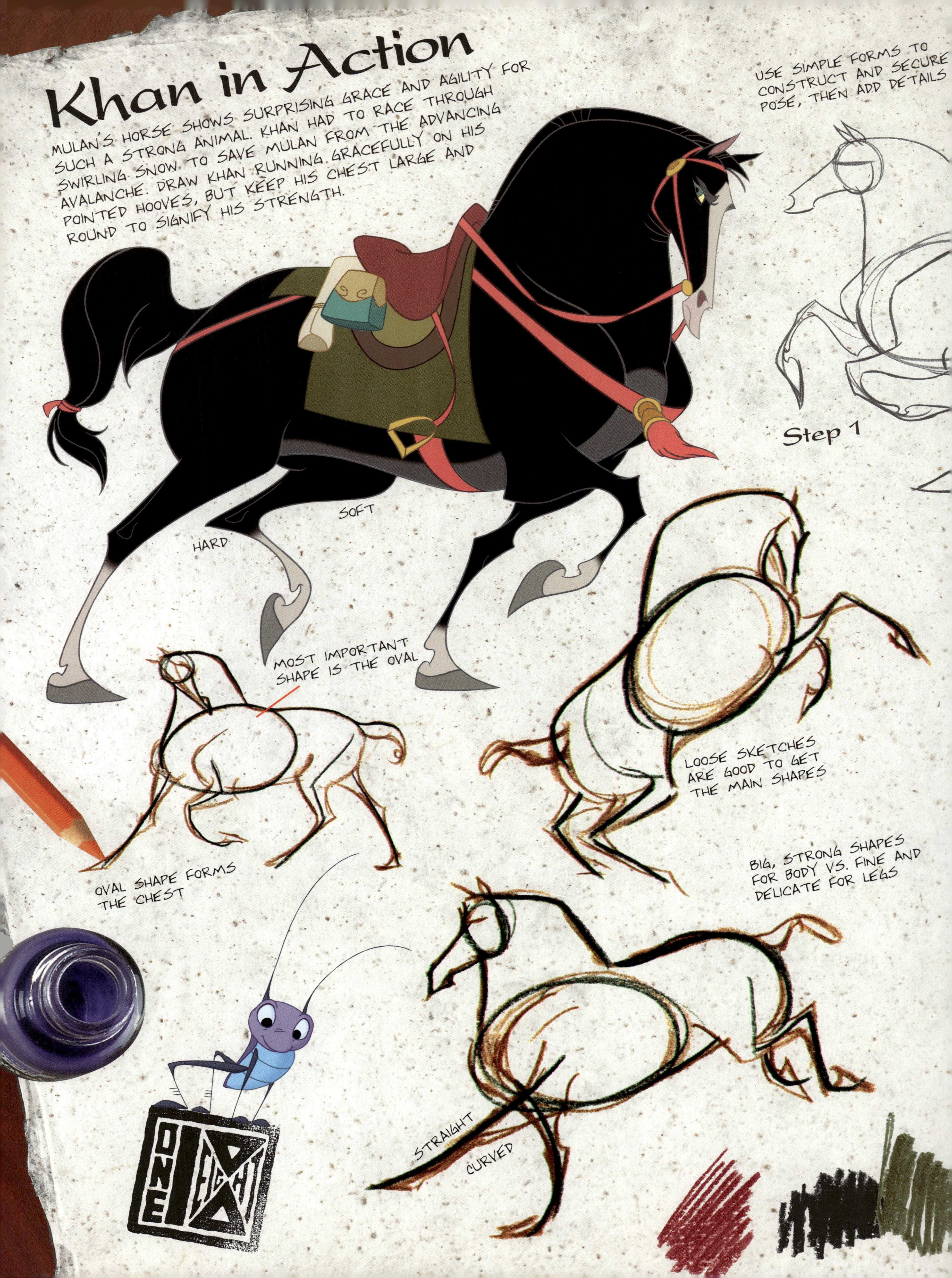

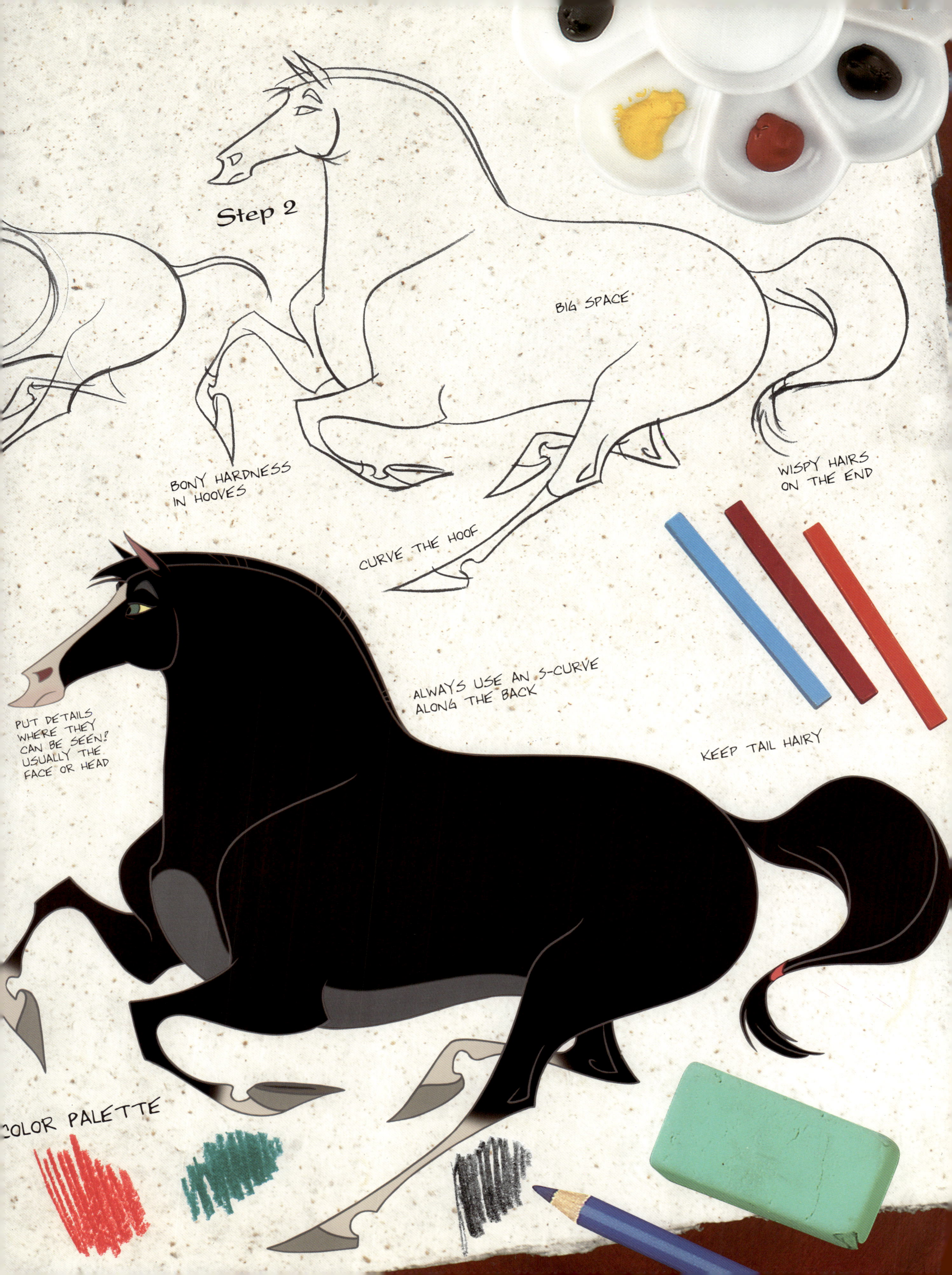
Step 2
BIG SPACE
BONY HARDNESS
IN HOOVES
WISPY HAIRS
ON THE END
CURVE THE HOOF
ALWAYS USE AN S-CURVE
ALONG THE BACK
PUT DETAILS
WHERE THEY
CAN BE SEEN!
USUALLY THE
FACE OR HEAD
KEEP TAIL HAIRY
COLOR PALETTE

Shang

AT THE SAME TIME MULAN IS ACTING OUT OF LOVE FOR HER FATHER, SHANG IS TRYING TO PROVE HIMSELF TO HIS OWN FATHER. HE WANTS TO SHOW GENERAL LI THAT HE WILL MAKE A GOOD COMMANDING OFFICER. HE HAS BEEN TRAINED AS A SOLDIER, BUT BENEATH HIS MUSCULAR CHEST BEATS A SYMPATHETIC HEART. TRY TO SHOW DETERMINATION AND KINDNESS IN SHANG'S EYES WHEN YOU DRAW HIS FACE. USE SMALL, GRAPHIC SHAPES TO CREATE HIS SIMPLE FEATURES.

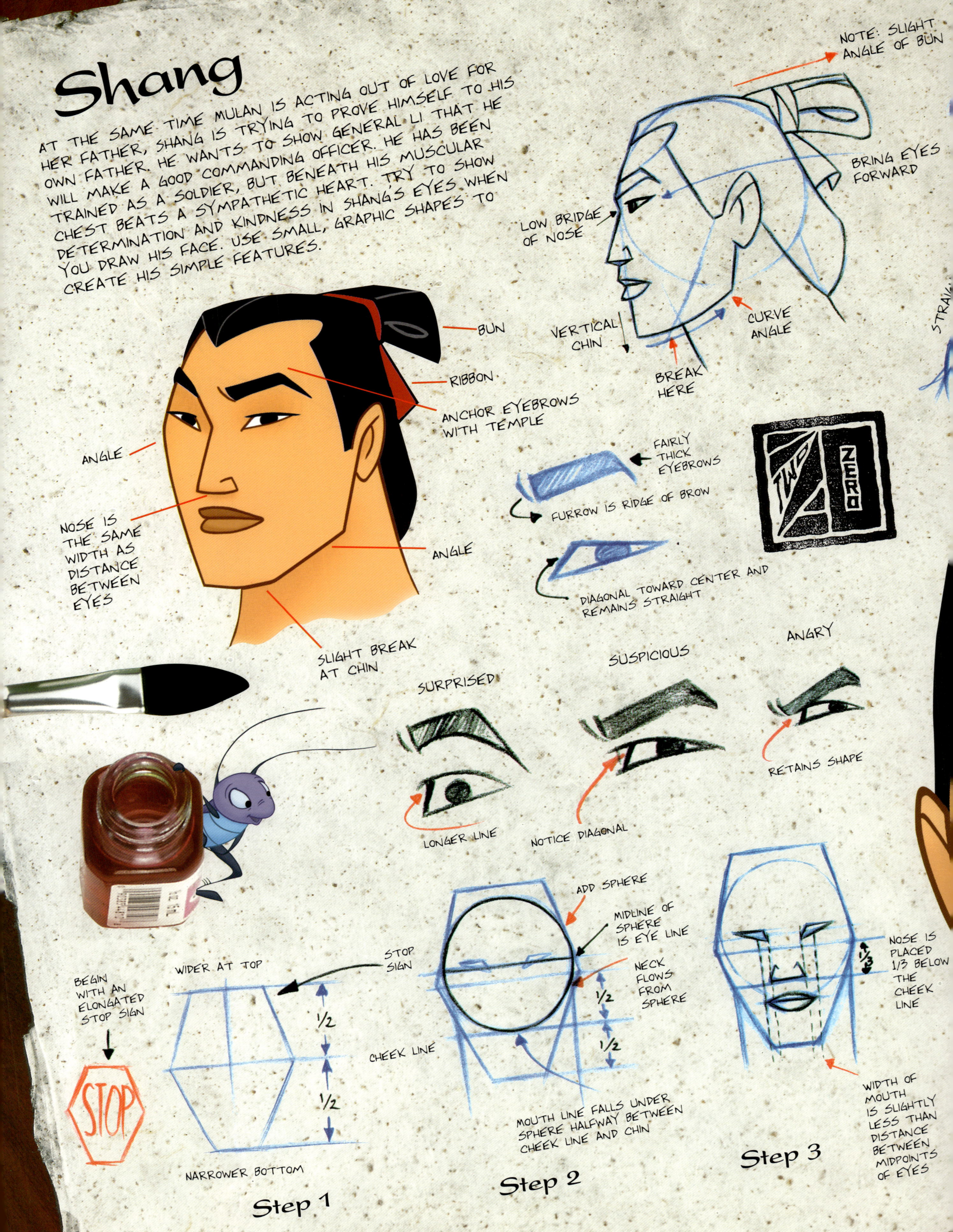

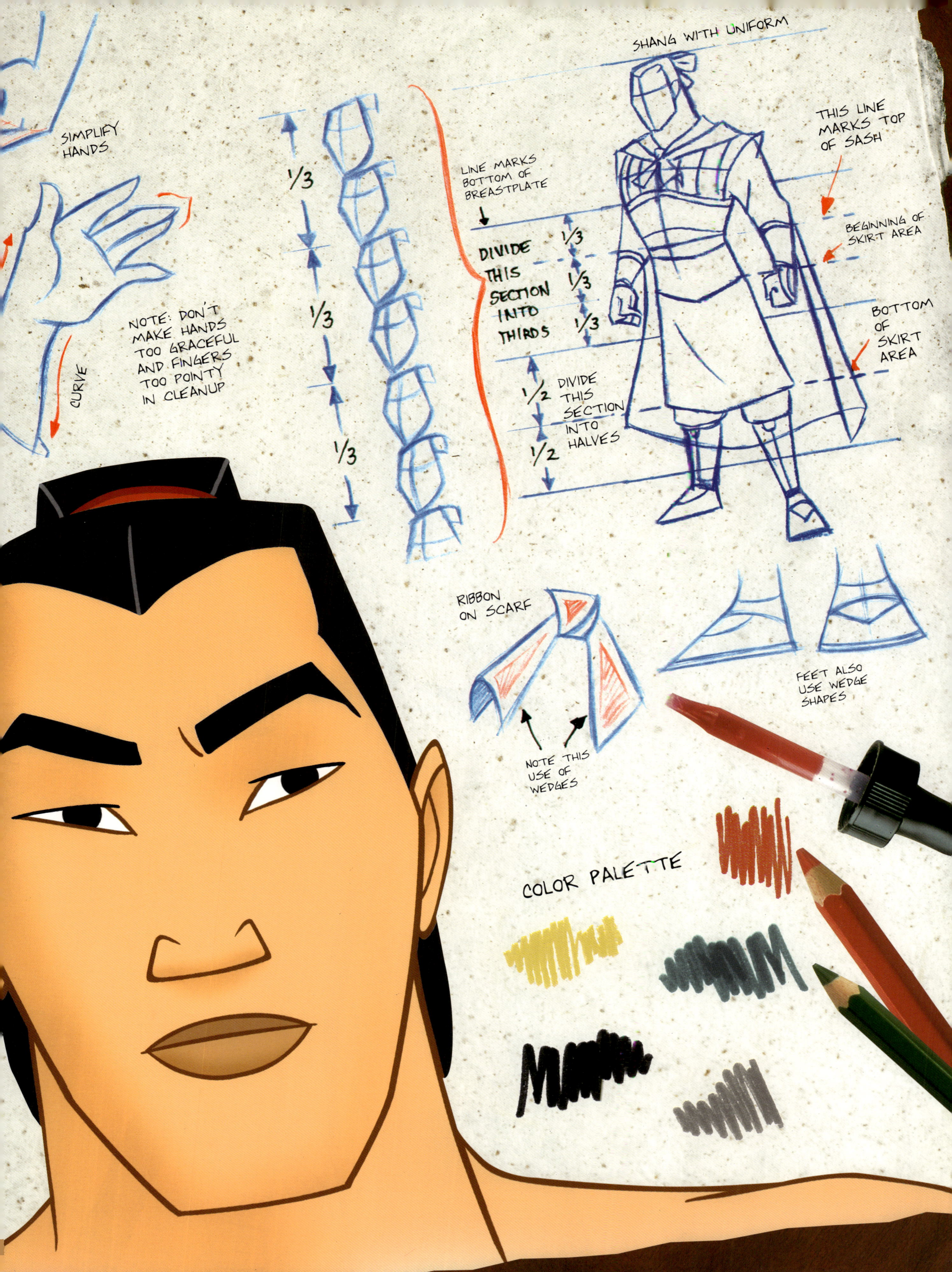

SIMPLIFY HANDS
NOTE: DON'T MAKE HANDS TOO GRACEFUL AND FINGERS TOO POINTY IN CLEANUP
CURVE
1/3
1/3
1/3
SHANG WITH UNIFORM
LINE MARKS BOTTOM OF BREASTPLATE
DIVIDE THIS SECTION INTO THIRDS
1/3
1/3
1/3
DIVIDE THIS SECTION INTO HALVES
1/2
1/2
THIS LINE MARKS TOP OF SASH
BEGINNING OF SKIRT AREA
BOTTOM OF SKIRT AREA
RIBBON ON SCARF
NOTE THIS USE OF WEDGES
FEET ALSO USE WEDGE SHAPES
COLOR PALETTE

Shang in Action

Shang has been trained in combat and martial arts, and his muscular body shows it. Using his hands as weapons, Shang is a skilled fighter. Try to capture the power and grace of his movements. Start with a simple shape, and then add details as you go.

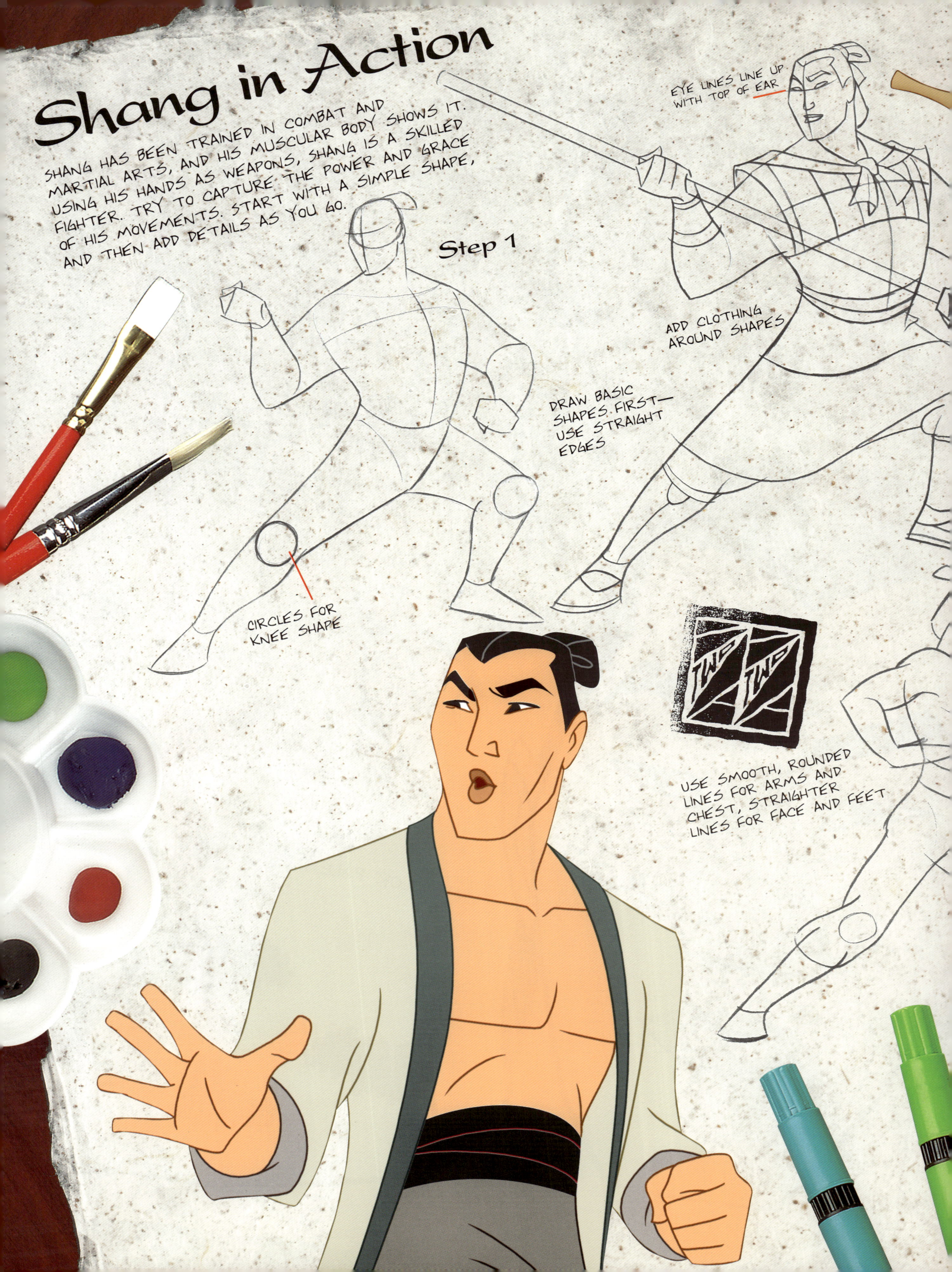

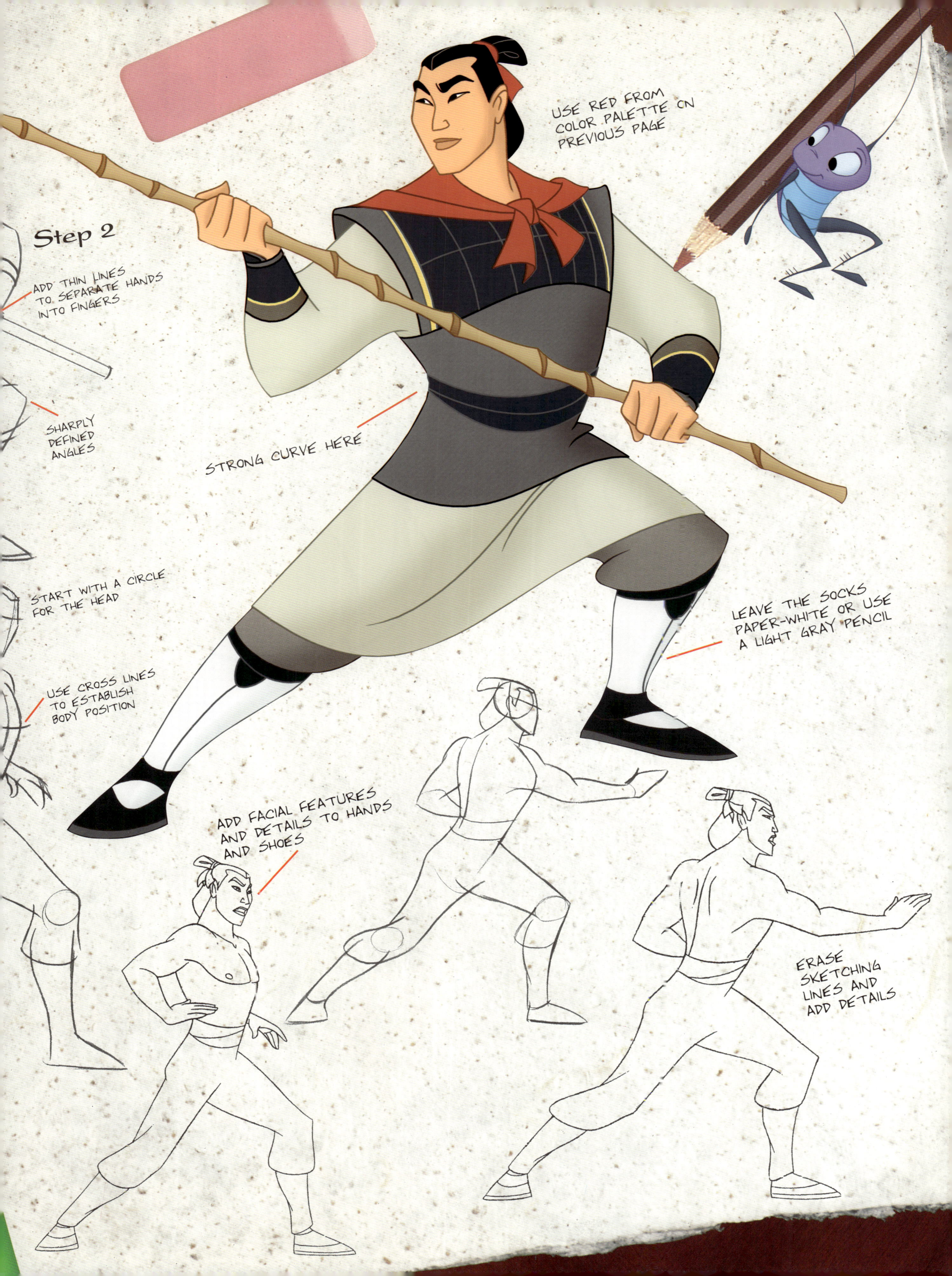

Step 2
ADD THIN LINES TO SEPARATE HANDS INTO FINGERS
SHARPLY DEFINED ANGLES
START WITH A CIRCLE FOR THE HEAD
USE CROSS LINES TO ESTABLISH BODY POSITION
USE RED FROM COLOR PALETTE ON PREVIOUS PAGE
STRONG CURVE HERE
LEAVE THE SOCKS PAPER-WHITE OR USE A LIGHT GRAY PENCIL
ADD FACIAL FEATURES AND DETAILS TO HANDS AND SHOES
ERASE SKETCHING LINES AND ADD DETAILS

Yao

Yao is a firecracker, and the slightest spark sets him off! This hot-tempered little man has an enormous chip on his shoulder, and he's always daring someone to knock it off in a fight. He takes a swing at Mulan on her first day in the army, and the brawl spreads throughout the troops. You can capture his personality by drawing him with a tough-guy scowl and a black eye, and be sure to draw his hand as a fist, ready to hit.

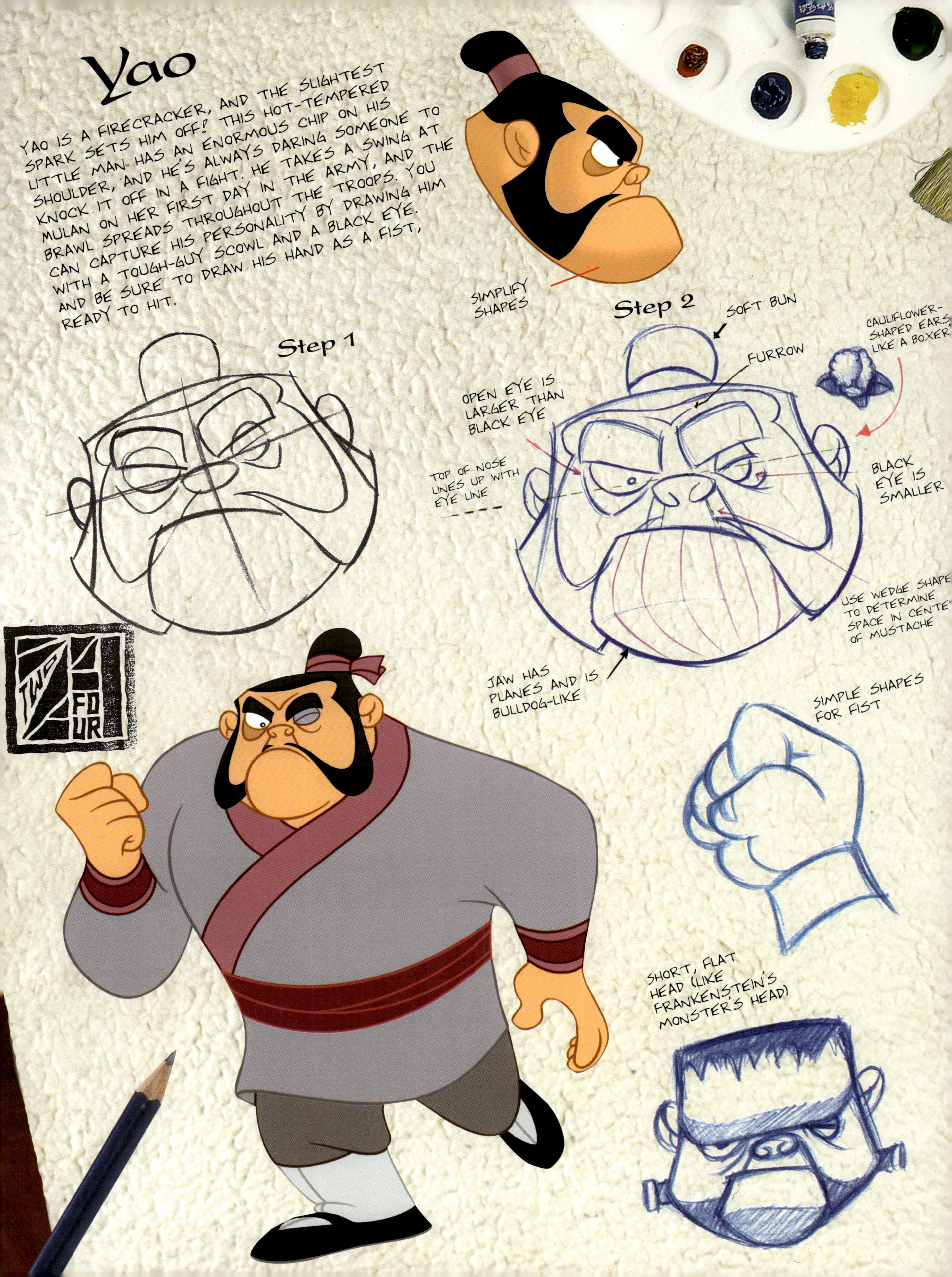

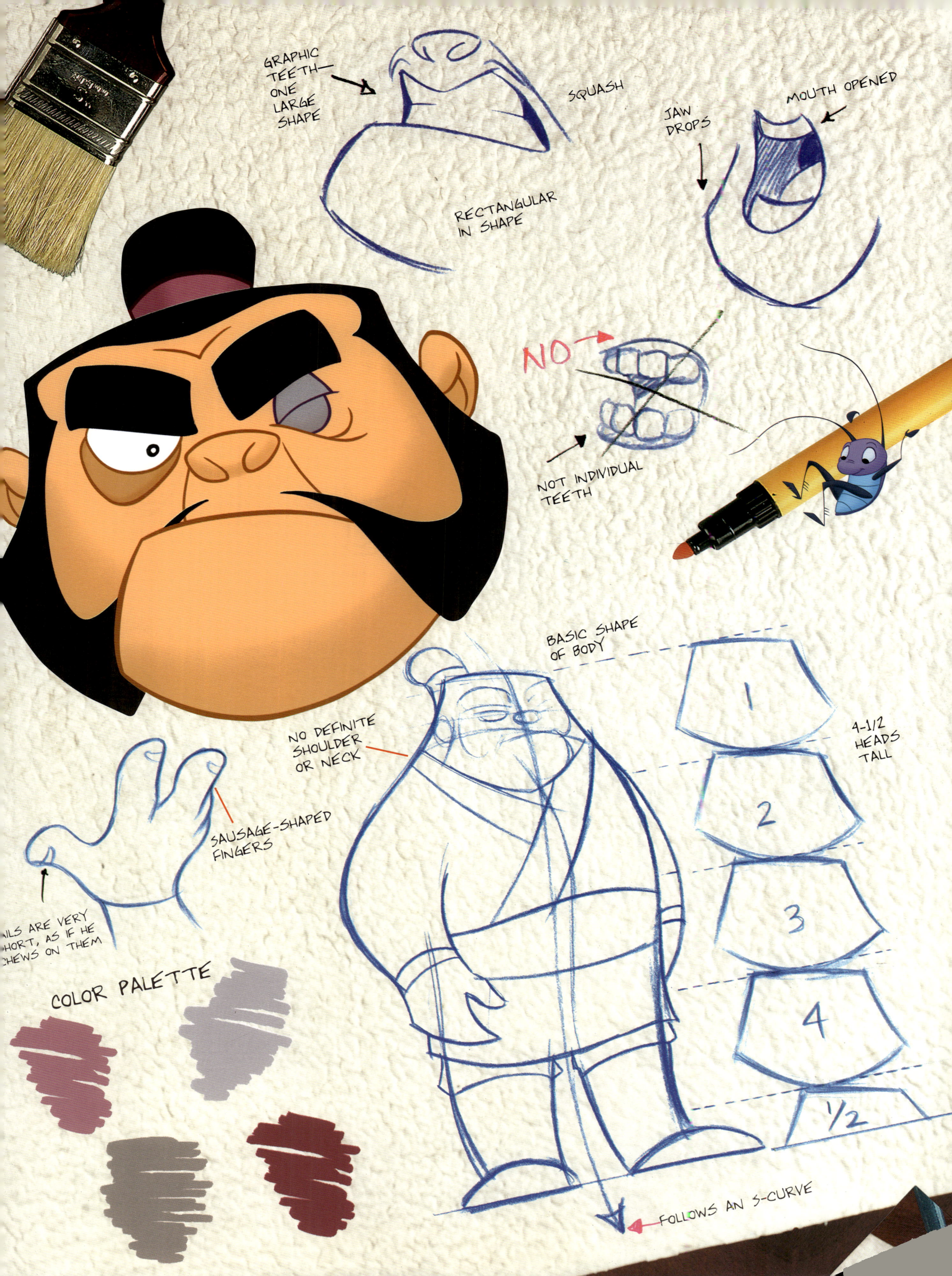
GRAPHIC TEETH— ONE LARGE SHAPE
SQUASH
RECTANGULAR IN SHAPE
JAW DROPS
MOUTH OPENED
NO
NOT INDIVIDUAL TEETH
BASIC SHAPE OF BODY
NO DEFINITE SHOULDER OR NECK
4-1/2 HEADS TALL
1
2
3
4
1/2
SAUSAGE-SHAPED FINGERS
NAILS ARE VERY SHORT, AS IF HE CHEWS ON THEM
COLOR PALETTE
FOLLOWS AN S-CURVE

Ling

LING WANTS TO MAKE FRIENDS WITH MULAN AS THEY ARE SWIMMING IN THE LAKE. BUT WHEN MUSHU COMES TO MULAN'S RESCUE BY BITING LING UNDERWATER, EVERYONE THINKS MUSHU IS A SNAKE. WHILE YOU WORK FROM THIS PAGE, YOU'LL NOTICE IT'S LING WHO IS THIN AND RUBBERY LIKE A SNAKE! ANIMATORS HAVE DRAWN LING'S LONG, FLEXIBLE BODY TO SUIT HIS COMIC ANTICS, AND THEY HAVE GIVEN HIM A GOOFY FACE TO MATCH. LING'S FEATURES ARE ALL BASED ON WEDGES—YOU'LL SEE THEM IN HIS NOSE, HIS CHEEKS, AND EVEN HIS EYEBROWS.

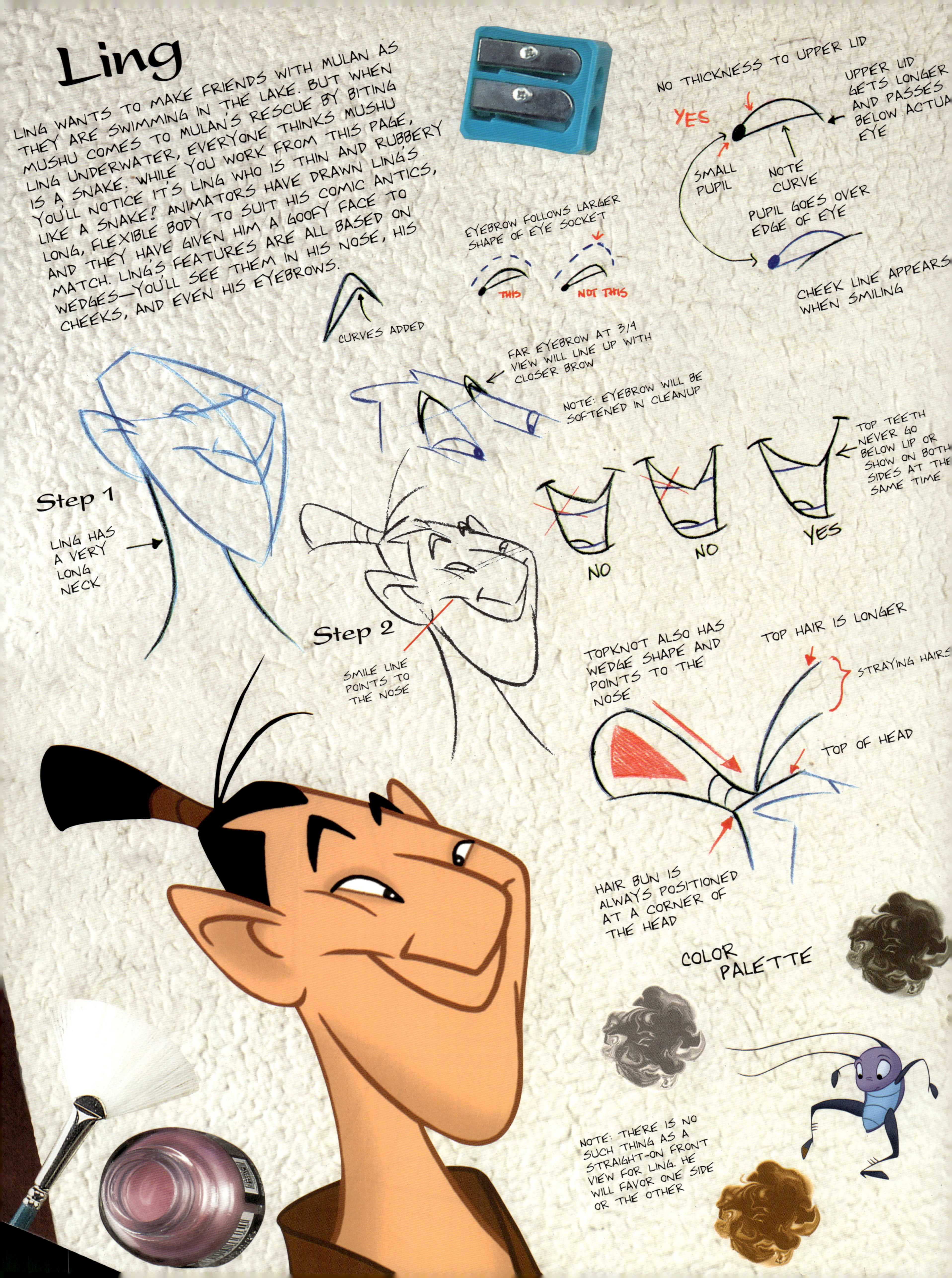

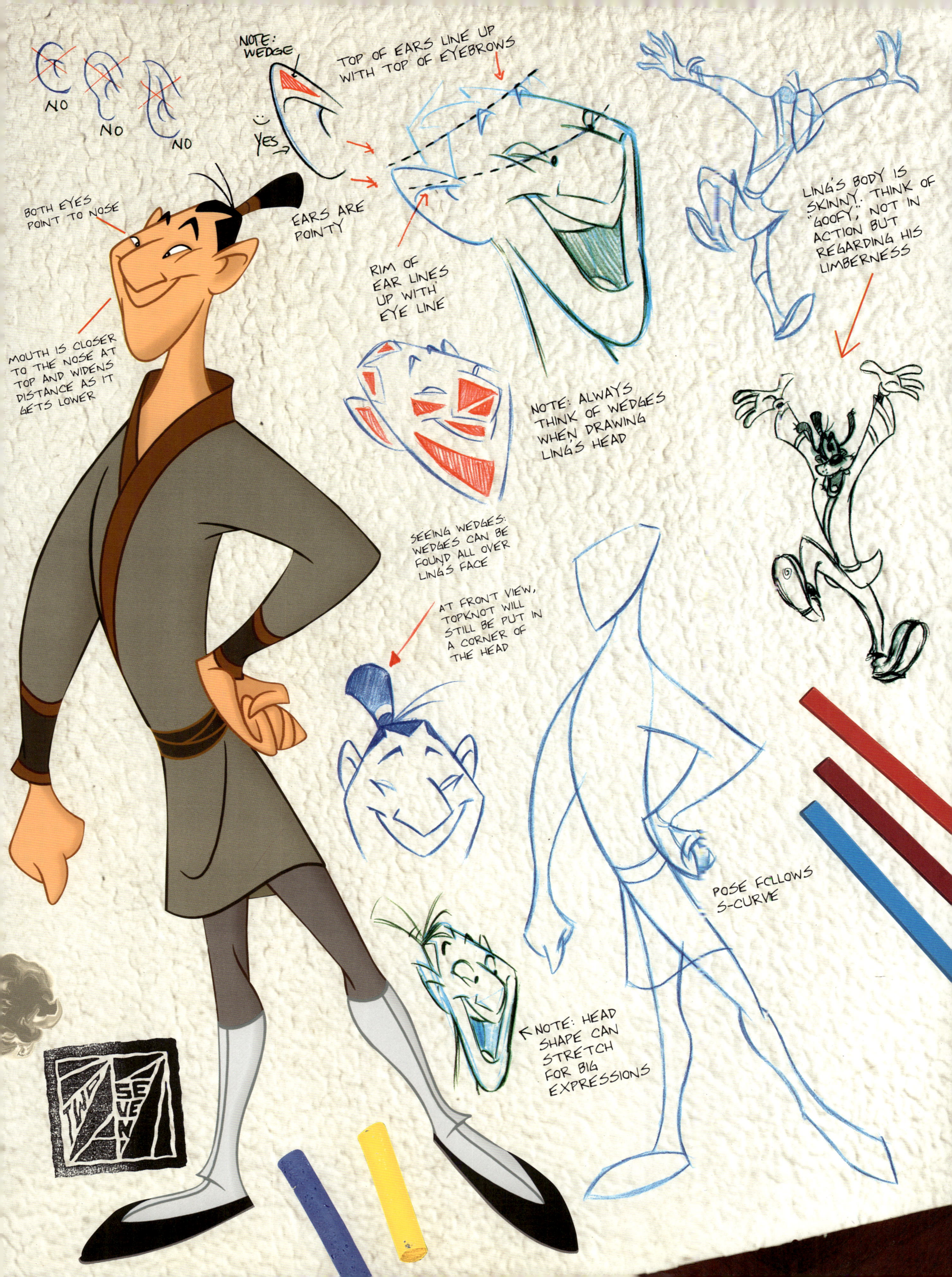
NO
NO
NO
NOTE: WEDGE
YES
TOP OF EARS LINE UP WITH TOP OF EYEBROWS
EARS ARE POINTY
RIM OF EAR LINES UP WITH EYE LINE
BOTH EYES POINT TO NOSE
MOUTH IS CLOSER TO THE NOSE AT TOP AND WIDENS DISTANCE AS IT GETS LOWER
LING'S BODY IS SKINNY. THINK OF "GOOFY," NOT IN ACTION BUT REGARDING HIS LIMBERNESS
NOTE: ALWAYS THINK OF WEDGES WHEN DRAWING LING'S HEAD
SEEING WEDGES: WEDGES CAN BE FOUND ALL OVER LING'S FACE
AT FRONT VIEW, TOPKNOT WILL STILL BE PUT IN A CORNER OF THE HEAD
POSE FOLLOWS S-CURVE
NOTE: HEAD SHAPE CAN STRETCH FOR BIG EXPRESSIONS
TWO
SEVEN

Chien-Po

IT TAKES A LOT TO GET CHIEN-PO EXCITED. CALM, CENTERED, AND CONTENT, HE'S THE OPPOSITE OF YAO. CHIEN-PO IS ALSO MORE THAN TWICE YAO'S SIZE! THE ONLY SMALL THING ABOUT HIM IS HIS SMILING MOUTH. THIS GENTLE GIANT IS AS STRONG AS AN ELEPHANT AND USES HIS MIGHT TO PULL SHANG, MULAN, AND HER COHORTS TO SAFETY IN THE AVALANCHE. TRY TO CAPTURE HIS BULKY STRENGTH BY USING CIRCULAR SHAPES FOR HIS BODY, HEAD, AND ARMS. AND THINK BIG!

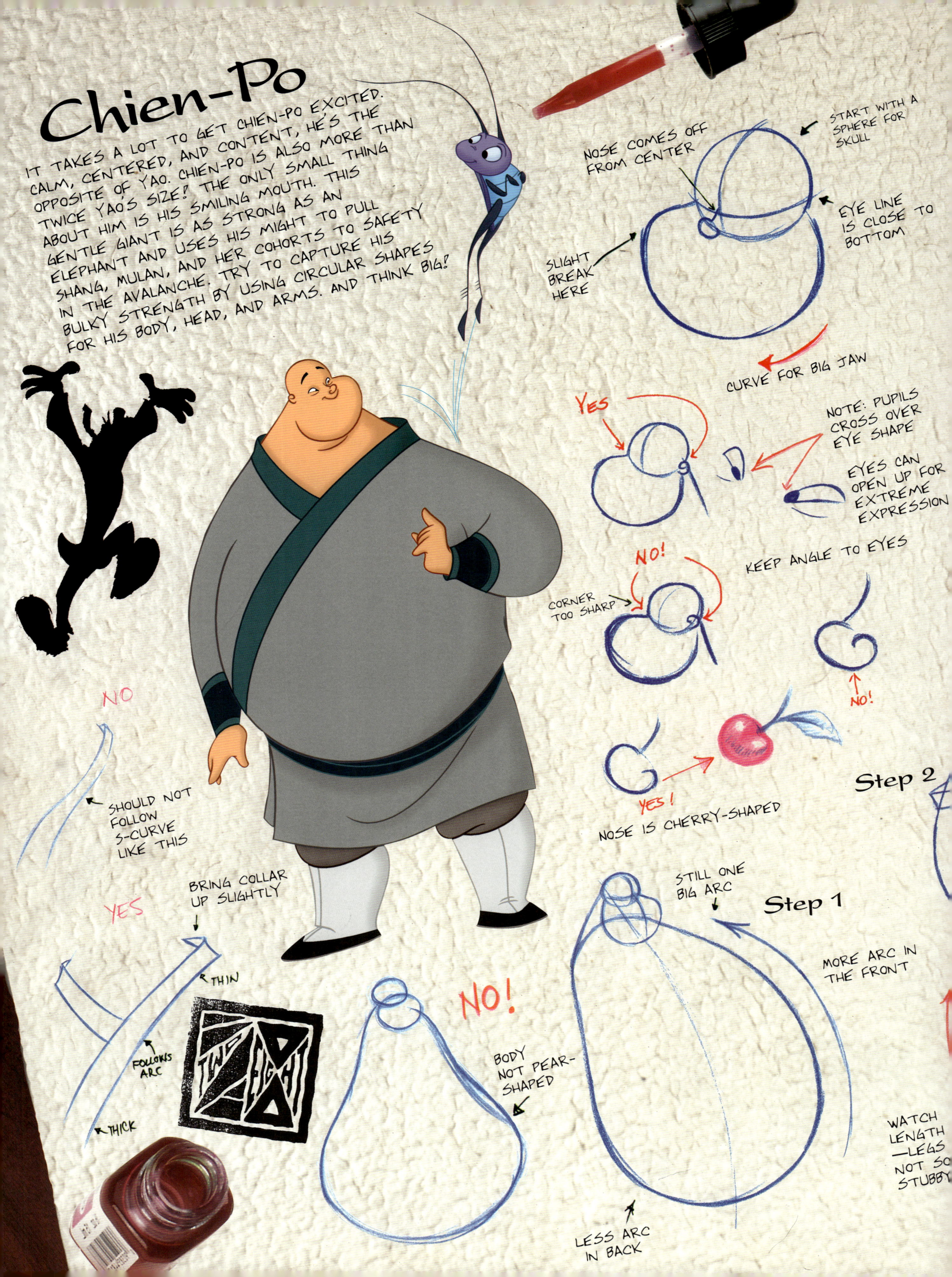

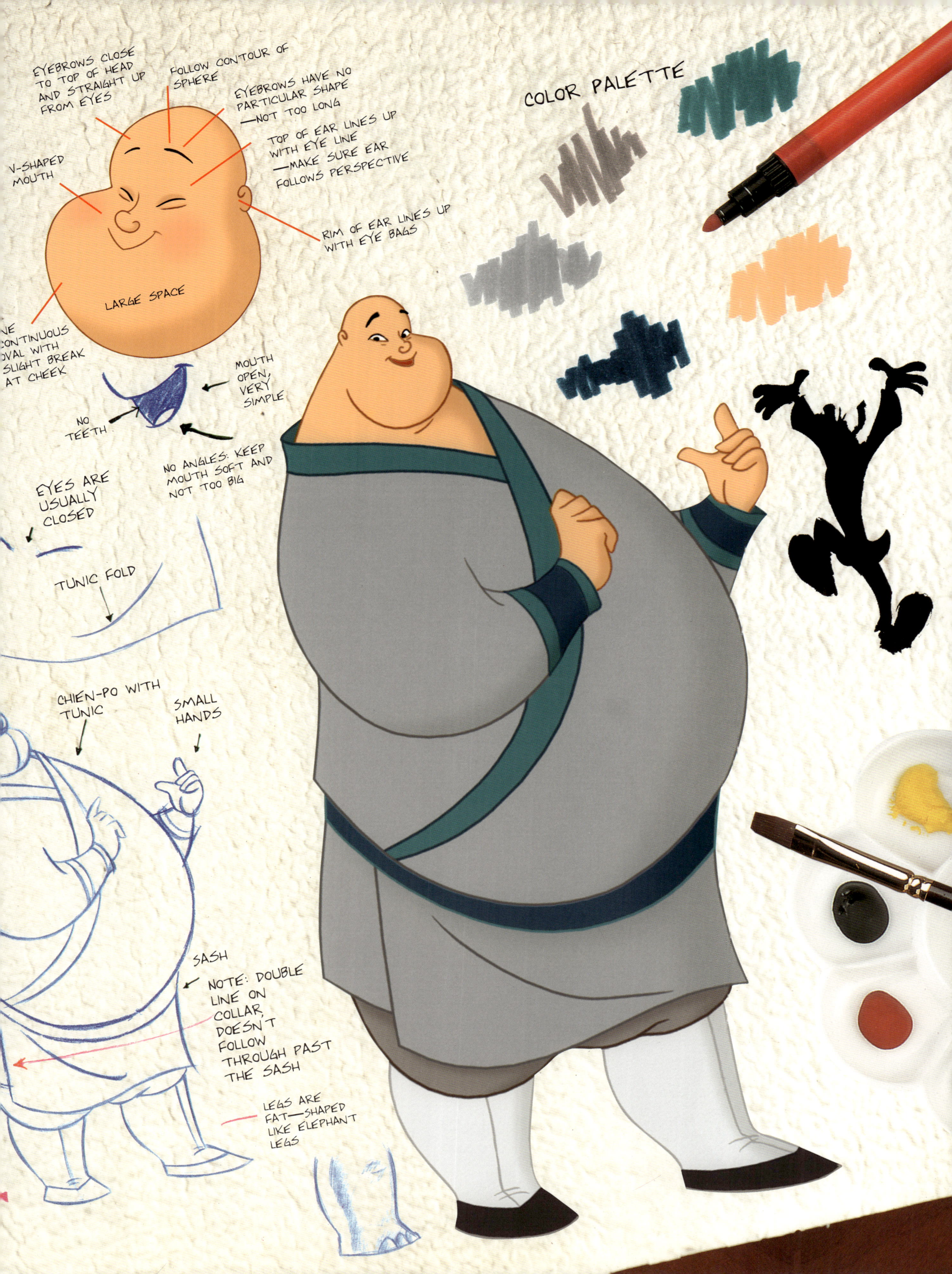
EYEBROWS CLOSE TO TOP OF HEAD AND STRAIGHT UP FROM EYES
FOLLOW CONTOUR OF SPHERE
EYEBROWS HAVE NO PARTICULAR SHAPE —NOT TOO LONG
TOP OF EAR LINES UP WITH EYE LINE —MAKE SURE EAR FOLLOWS PERSPECTIVE
V-SHAPED MOUTH
RIM OF EAR LINES UP WITH EYE BAGS
LARGE SPACE
CONTINUOUS OVAL WITH SLIGHT BREAK AT CHEEK
MOUTH OPEN, VERY SIMPLE
NO TEETH
NO ANGLES: KEEP MOUTH SOFT AND NOT TOO BIG
EYES ARE USUALLY CLOSED
TUNIC FOLD
COLOR PALETTE
CHIEN-PO WITH TUNIC
SMALL HANDS
SASH
NOTE: DOUBLE LINE ON COLLAR, DOESN'T FOLLOW THROUGH PAST THE SASH
LEGS ARE FAT—SHAPED LIKE ELEPHANT LEGS

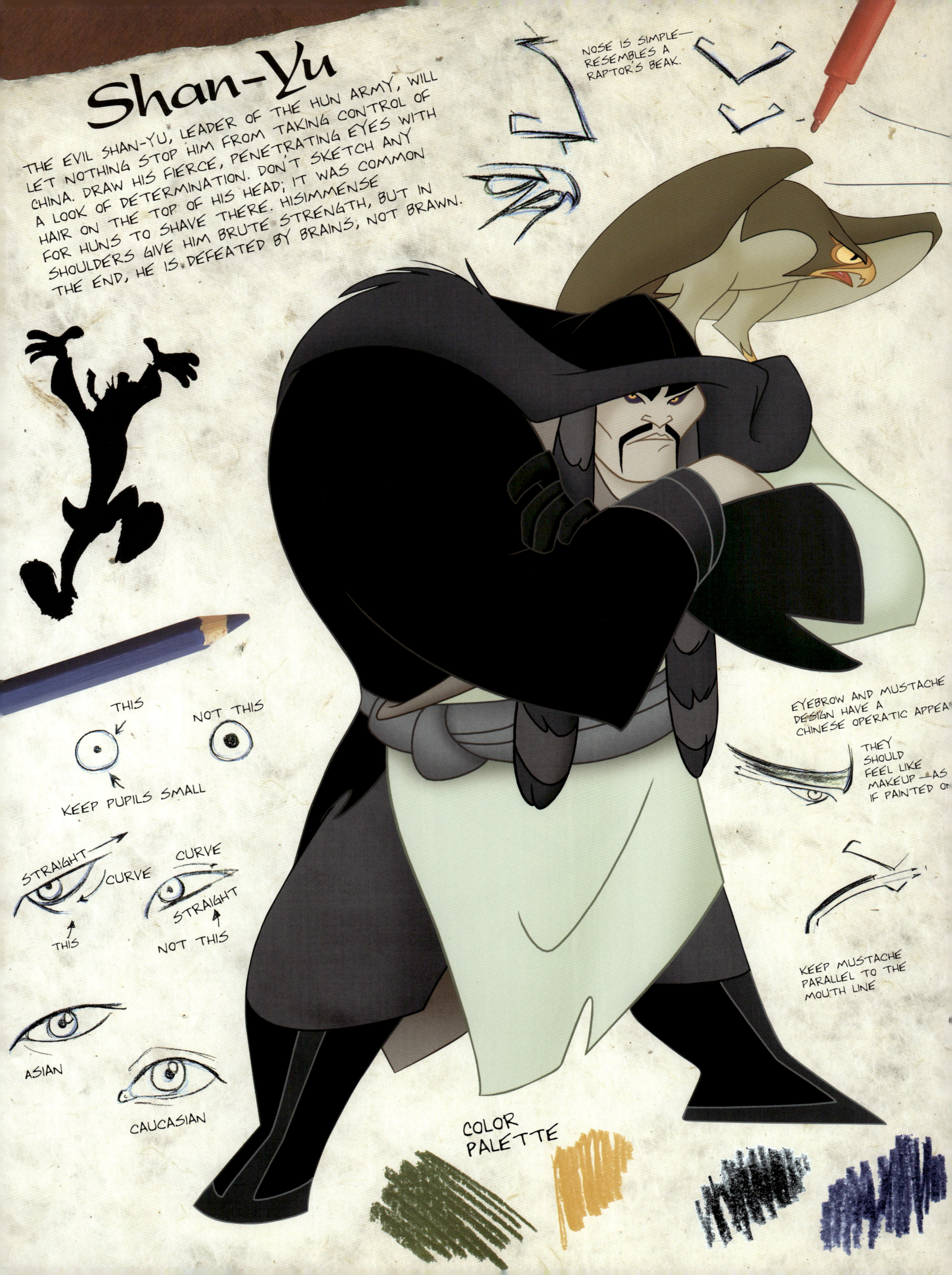
Shan-Yu
THE EVIL SHAN-YU, LEADER OF THE HUN ARMY, WILL LET NOTHING STOP HIM FROM TAKING CONTROL OF CHINA. DRAW HIS FIERCE, PENETRATING EYES WITH A LOOK OF DETERMINATION. DON'T SKETCH ANY HAIR ON THE TOP OF HIS HEAD; IT WAS COMMON FOR HUNS TO SHAVE THERE. HISIMMENSE SHOULDERS GIVE HIM BRUTE STRENGTH, BUT IN THE END, HE IS DEFEATED BY BRAINS, NOT BRAWN.
NOSE IS SIMPLE—RESEMBLES A RAPTOR'S BEAK.
THIS
NOT THIS
KEEP PUPILS SMALL
STRAIGHT
CURVE
THIS
CURVE
STRAIGHT
NOT THIS
ASIAN
CAUCASIAN
EYEBROW AND MUSTACHE DESIGN HAVE A CHINESE OPERATIC APPEA
THEY SHOULD FEEL LIKE MAKEUP—AS IF PAINTED O
KEEP MUSTACHE PARALLEL TO THE MOUTH LINE
COLOR PALETTE

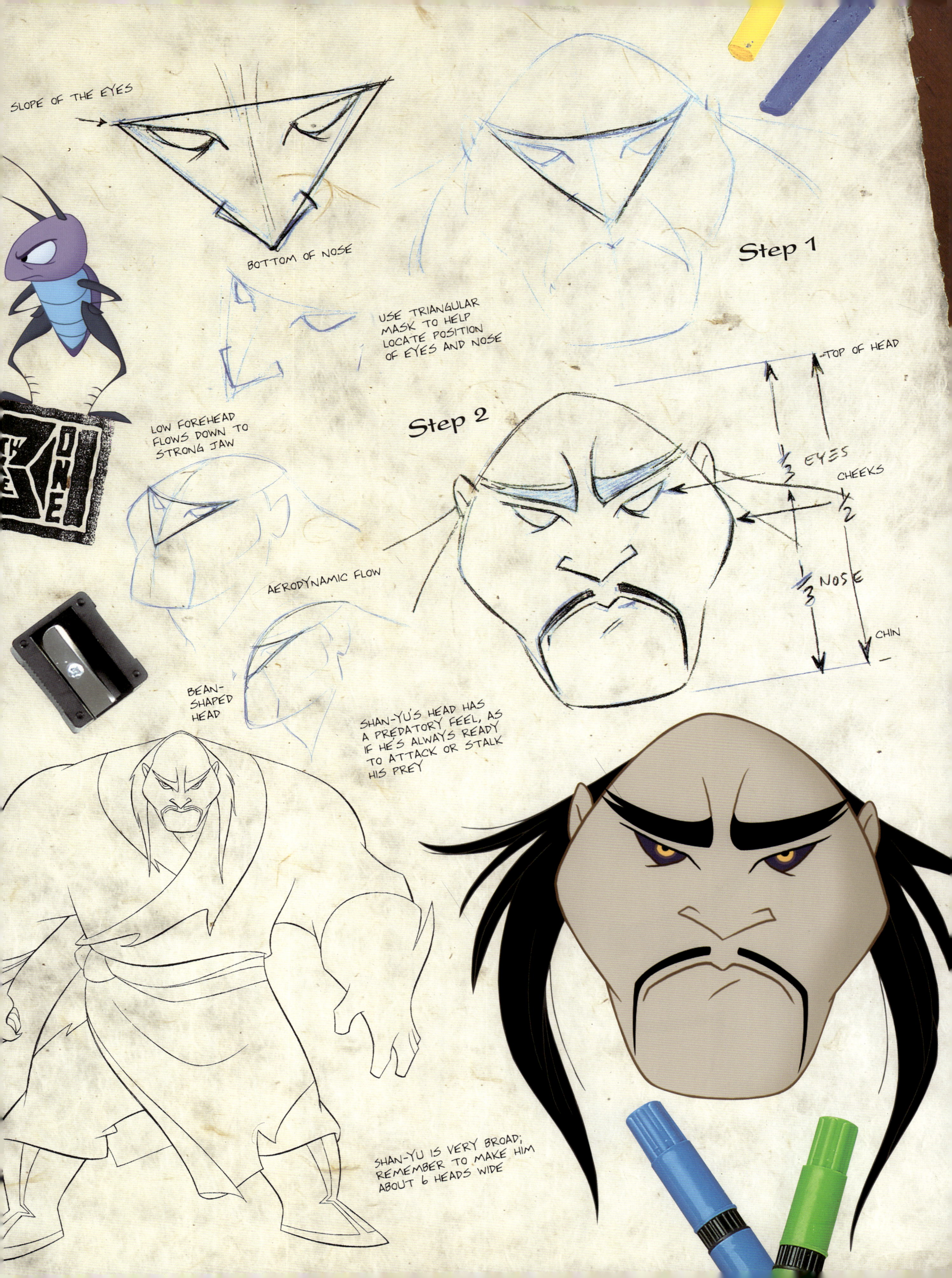
SLOPE OF THE EYES
BOTTOM OF NOSE
USE TRIANGULAR MASK TO HELP LOCATE POSITION OF EYES AND NOSE
Step 1
Step 2
TOP OF HEAD
EYES
CHEEKS
NOSE
CHIN
LOW FOREHEAD FLOWS DOWN TO STRONG JAW
AERODYNAMIC FLOW
BEAN-SHAPED HEAD
SHAN-YU'S HEAD HAS A PREDATORY FEEL, AS IF HE'S ALWAYS READY TO ATTACK OR STALK HIS PREY
SHAN-YU IS VERY BROAD; REMEMBER TO MAKE HIM ABOUT 6 HEADS WIDE

Shan-Yu in Action

IN BATTLE, SHAN-YU HAS THE STRENGTH OF TEN MEN. HE CAN WIELD THE LARGEST SWORD WITH EASE AND BRUSH OFF BLOWS AS IF THEY WERE SNOWFLAKES. USUALLY PERCHED ON HIS HUGE SHOULDER IS HIS TRUSTY FALCON, ANOTHER PREDATOR WHO PREYS ON THE WEAK. DRAW SHAN-YU'S HULKING FIGURE WITH AN EXAGGERATED CHEST AND STOCKY THIGHS.

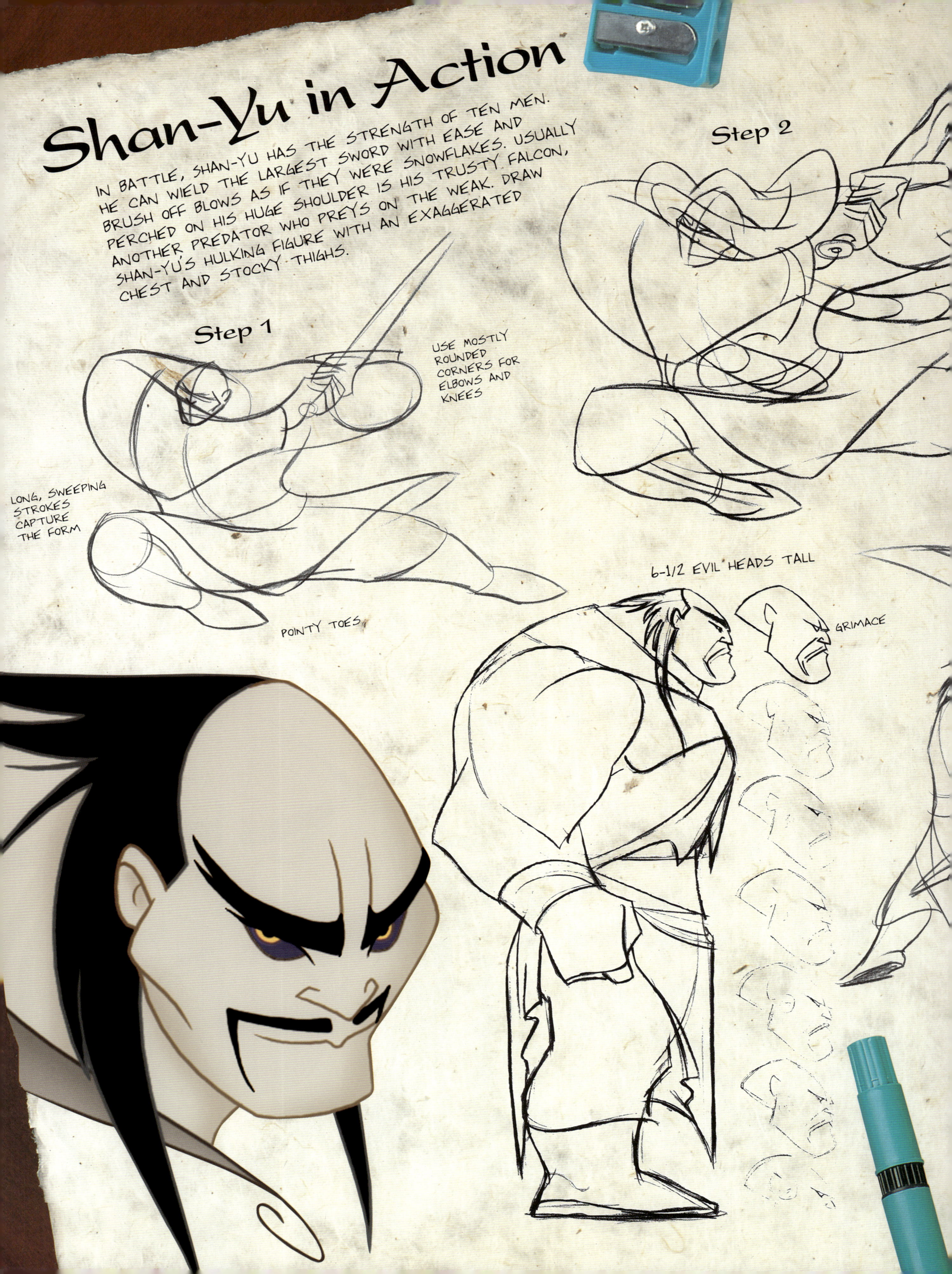

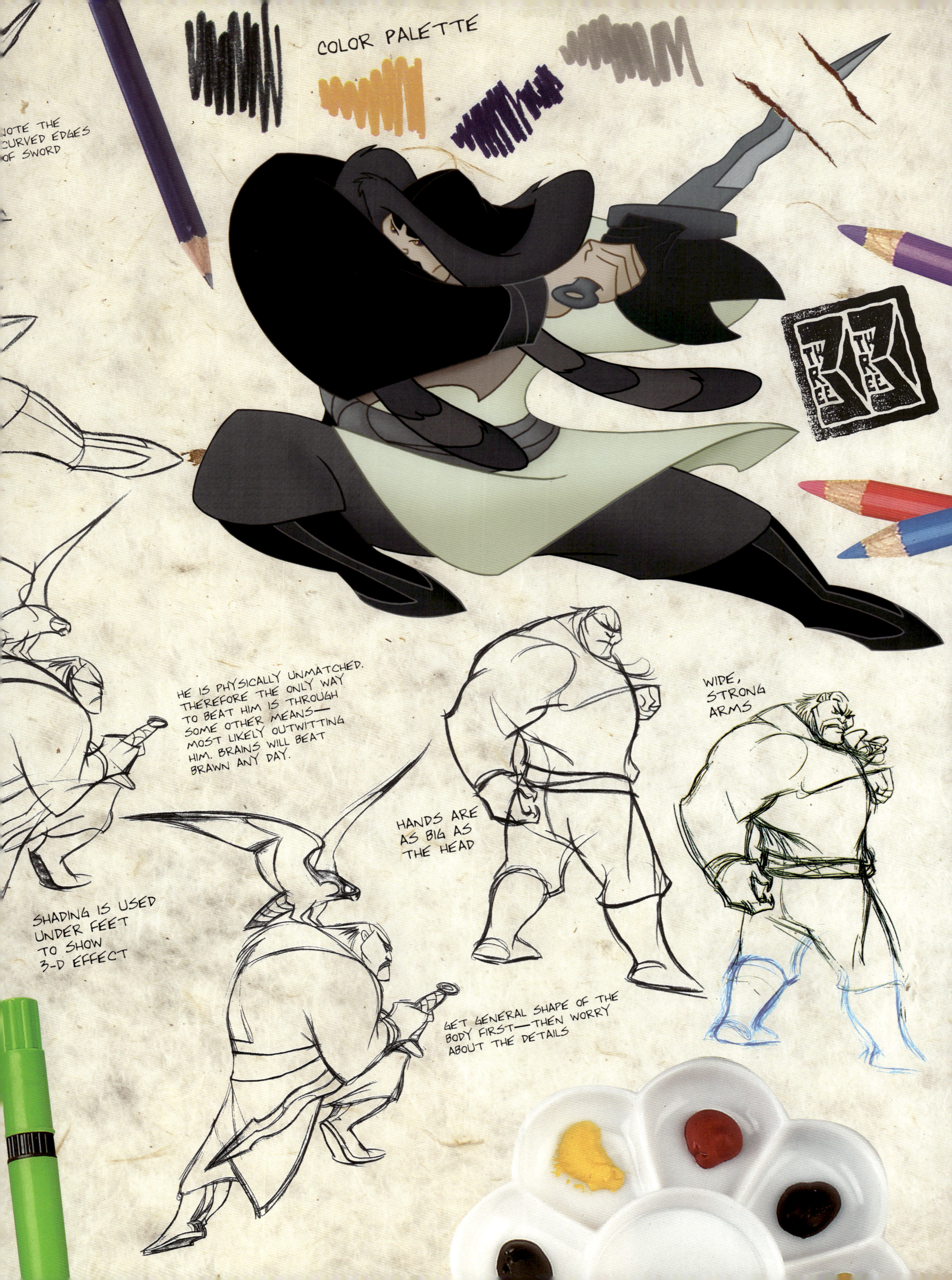
COLOR PALETTE
NOTE THE CURVED EDGES OF SWORD
HE IS PHYSICALLY UNMATCHED. THEREFORE THE ONLY WAY TO BEAT HIM IS THROUGH SOME OTHER MEANS— MOST LIKELY OUTWITTING HIM. BRAINS WILL BEAT BRAWN ANY DAY.
WIDE, STRONG ARMS
HANDS ARE AS BIG AS THE HEAD
SHADING IS USED UNDER FEET TO SHOW 3-D EFFECT
GET GENERAL SHAPE OF THE BODY FIRST—THEN WORRY ABOUT THE DETAILS

Costumes

COSTUMES CAN CONVEY A LOT OF INFORMATION ABOUT AN INDIVIDUAL'S PERSONALITY, ACTIONS, AND EMOTIONS. ALTHOUGH COSTUMES COVER THE CHARACTERS' BODIES, THEY ALSO REVEAL MUCH ABOUT WHAT MAKES EACH PERSON UNIQUE.

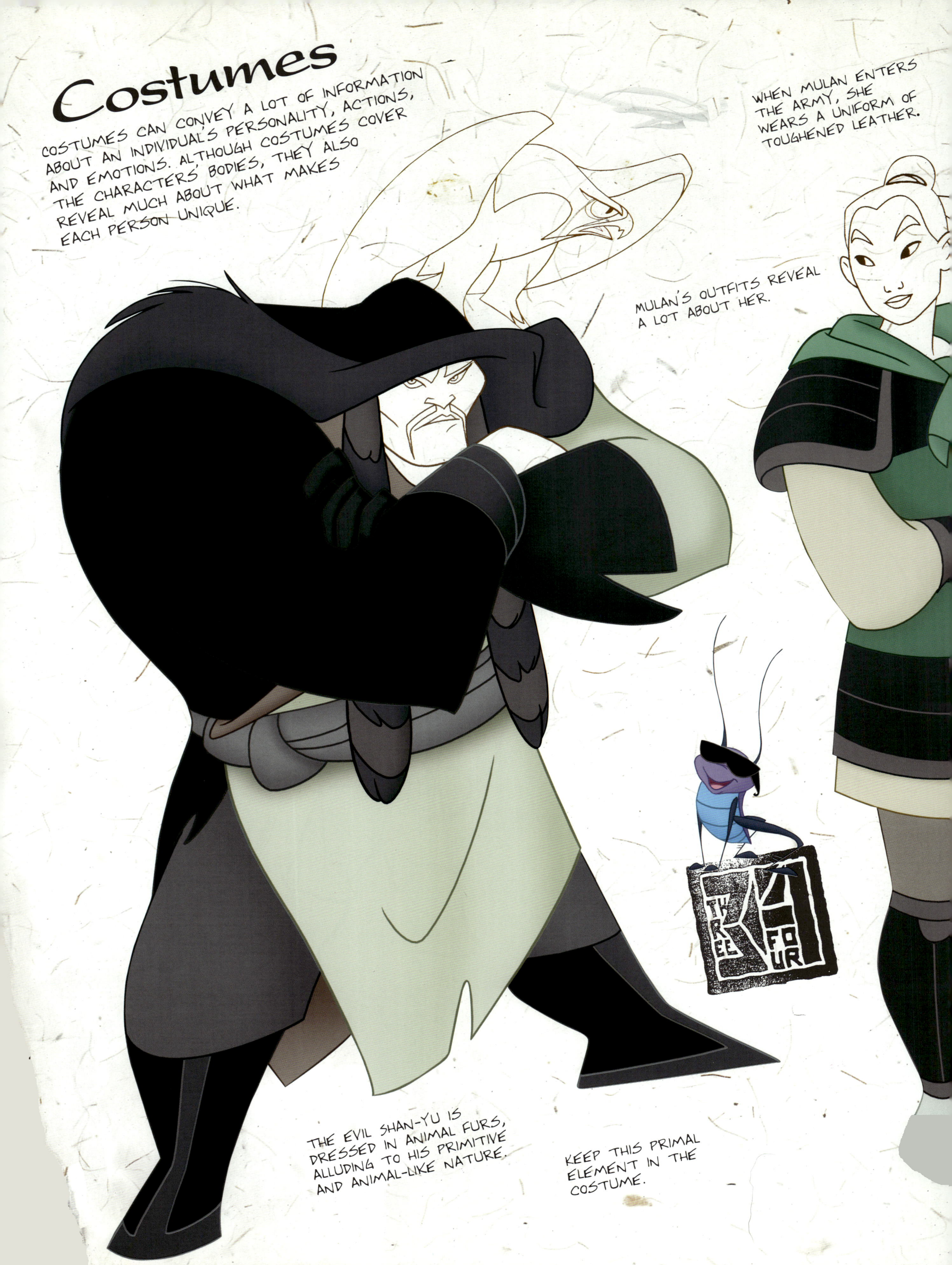

WHEN MULAN ENTERS THE ARMY, SHE WEARS A UNIFORM OF TOUGHENED LEATHER.

MULAN'S OUTFITS REVEAL A LOT ABOUT HER.

THE EVIL SHAN-YU IS DRESSED IN ANIMAL FURS, ALLUDING TO HIS PRIMITIVE AND ANIMAL-LIKE NATURE.

KEEP THIS PRIMAL ELEMENT IN THE COSTUME.

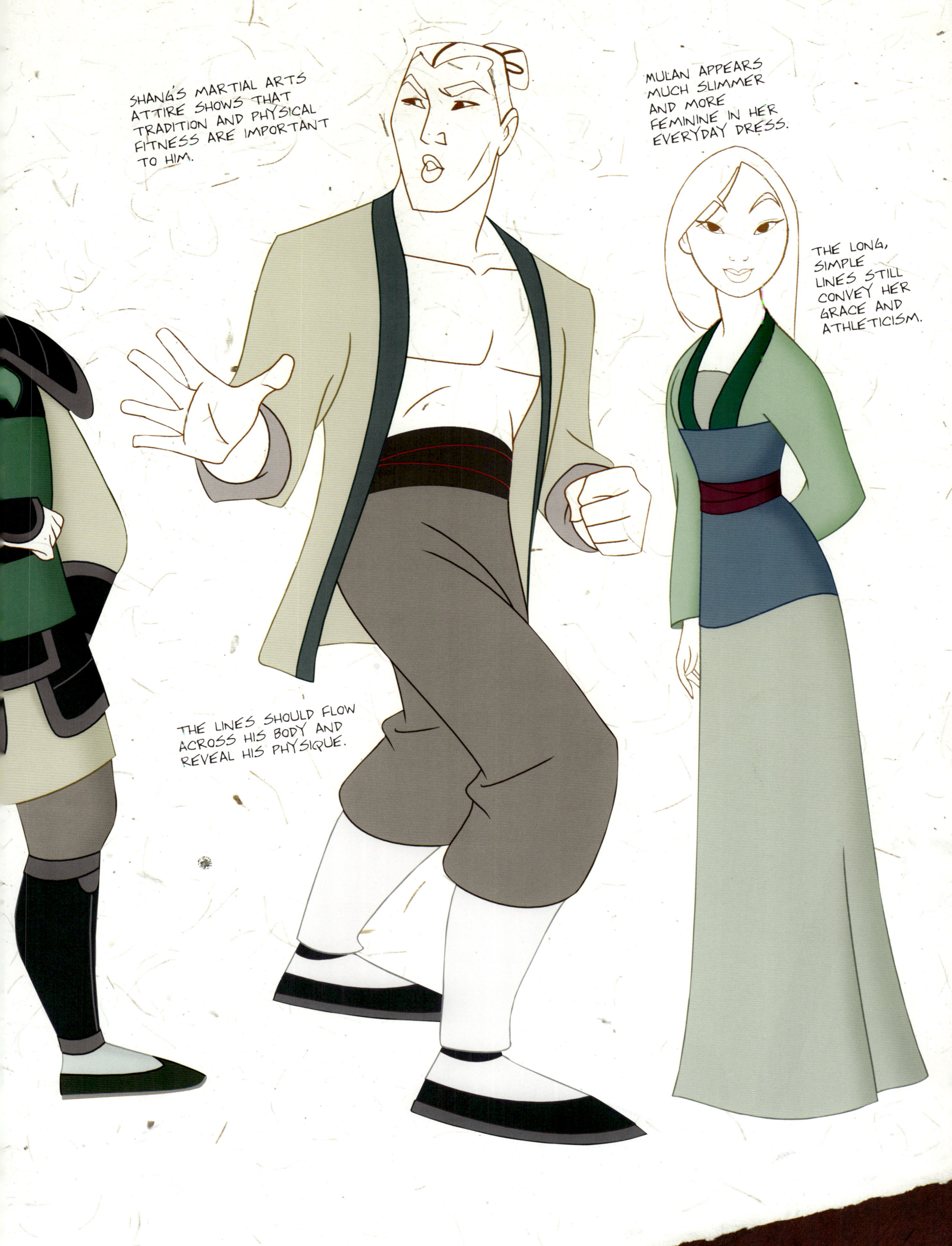
SHANG'S MARTIAL ARTS ATTIRE SHOWS THAT TRADITION AND PHYSICAL FITNESS ARE IMPORTANT TO HIM.
MULAN APPEARS MUCH SLIMMER AND MORE FEMININE IN HER EVERYDAY DRESS.
THE LONG, SIMPLE LINES STILL CONVEY HER GRACE AND ATHLETICISM.
THE LINES SHOULD FLOW ACROSS HIS BODY AND REVEAL HIS PHYSIQUE.

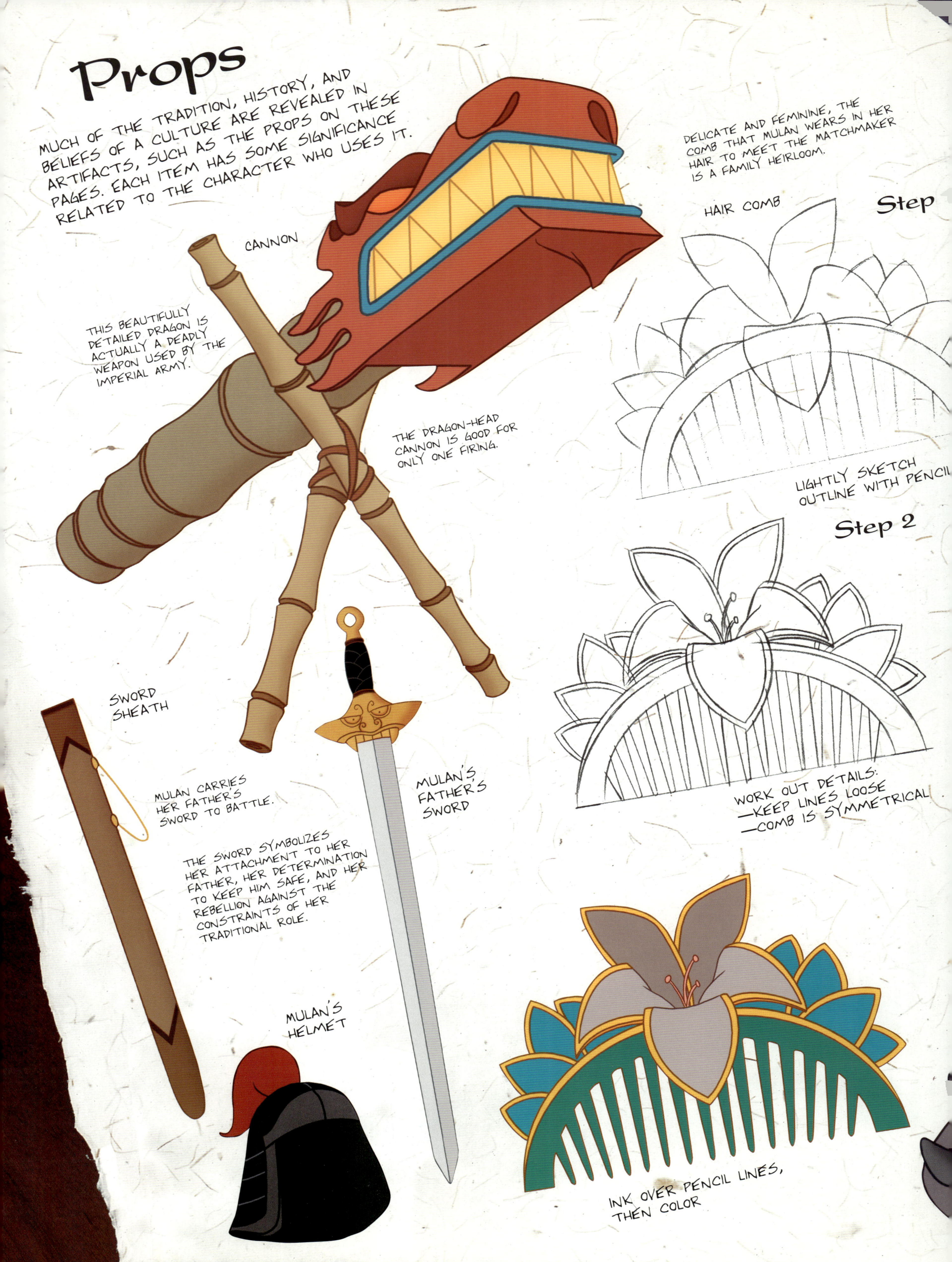
Props
MUCH OF THE TRADITION, HISTORY, AND BELIEFS OF A CULTURE ARE REVEALED IN ARTIFACTS, SUCH AS THE PROPS ON THESE PAGES. EACH ITEM HAS SOME SIGNIFICANCE RELATED TO THE CHARACTER WHO USES IT.
CANNON
THIS BEAUTIFULLY DETAILED DRAGON IS ACTUALLY A DEADLY WEAPON USED BY THE IMPERIAL ARMY.
THE DRAGON-HEAD CANNON IS GOOD FOR ONLY ONE FIRING.
DELICATE AND FEMININE, THE COMB THAT MULAN WEARS IN HER HAIR TO MEET THE MATCHMAKER IS A FAMILY HEIRLOOM.
HAIR COMB
Step
LIGHTLY SKETCH OUTLINE WITH PENCIL
Step 2
WORK OUT DETAILS:
—KEEP LINES LOOSE
—COMB IS SYMMETRICAL
SWORD SHEATH
MULAN CARRIES HER FATHER'S SWORD TO BATTLE.
MULAN'S FATHER'S SWORD
THE SWORD SYMBOLIZES HER ATTACHMENT TO HER FATHER, HER DETERMINATION TO KEEP HIM SAFE, AND HER REBELLION AGAINST THE CONSTRAINTS OF HER TRADITIONAL ROLE.
MULAN'S HELMET
INK OVER PENCIL LINES, THEN COLOR

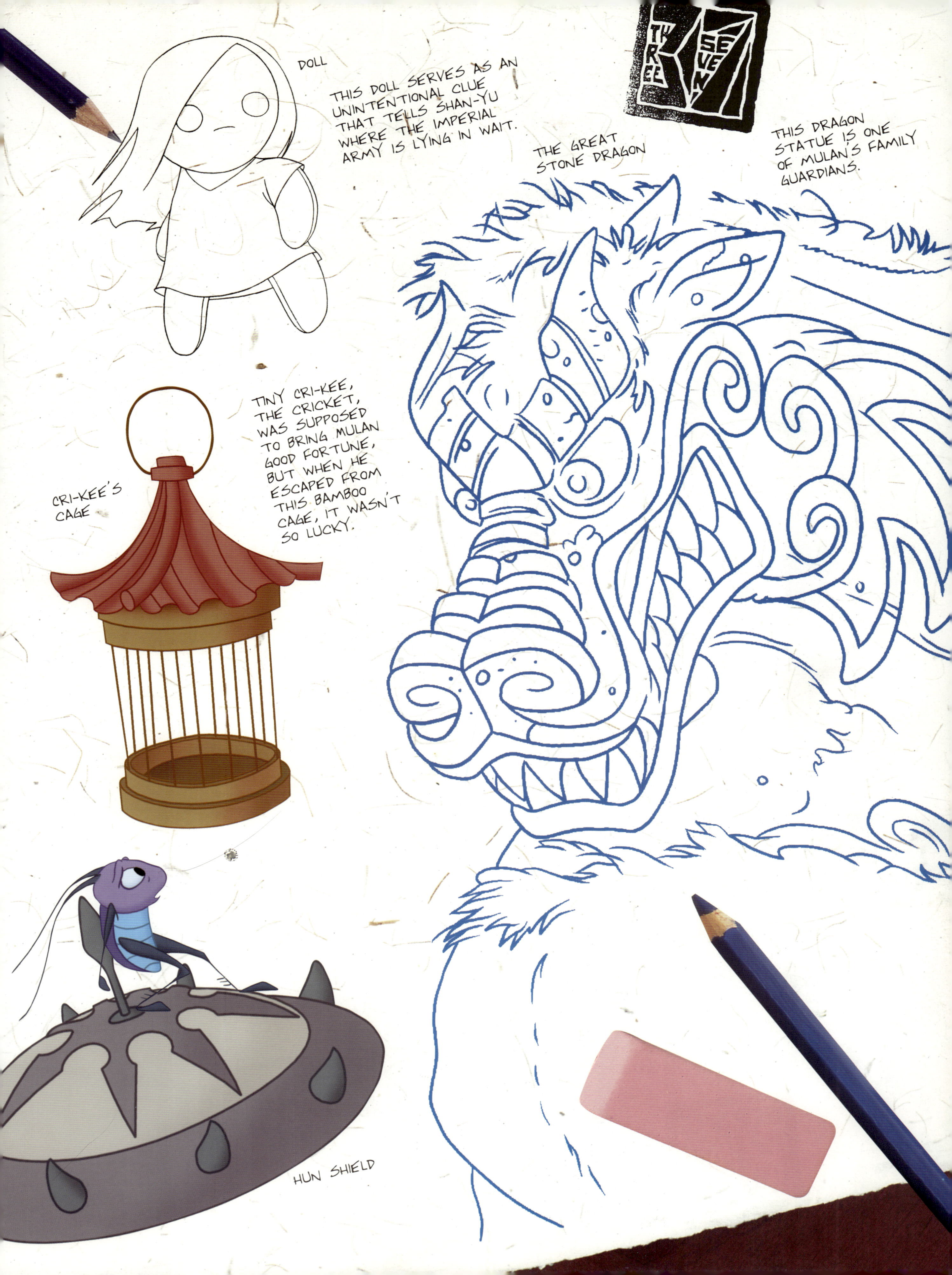

THREE
SEVEN
DOLL
THIS DOLL SERVES AS AN UNINTENTIONAL CLUE THAT TELLS SHAN-YU WHERE THE IMPERIAL ARMY IS LYING IN WAIT.
THE GREAT STONE DRAGON
THIS DRAGON STATUE IS ONE OF MULAN'S FAMILY GUARDIANS.
TINY CRI-KEE, THE CRICKET, WAS SUPPOSED TO BRING MULAN GOOD FORTUNE, BUT WHEN HE ESCAPED FROM THIS BAMBOO CAGE, IT WASN'T SO LUCKY.
CRI-KEE'S CAGE
HUN SHIELD

Creating a Scene

THE GUIDING DESIGN PRINCIPLE OF **MULAN** CAN BE DESCRIBED AS "POETIC SIMPLICITY." THIS THREE-PANEL BACKGROUND COMBINES THE DISTINCT LOOK OF TRADITIONAL CHINESE PAINTINGS WITH A WESTERN INTERPRETATION.

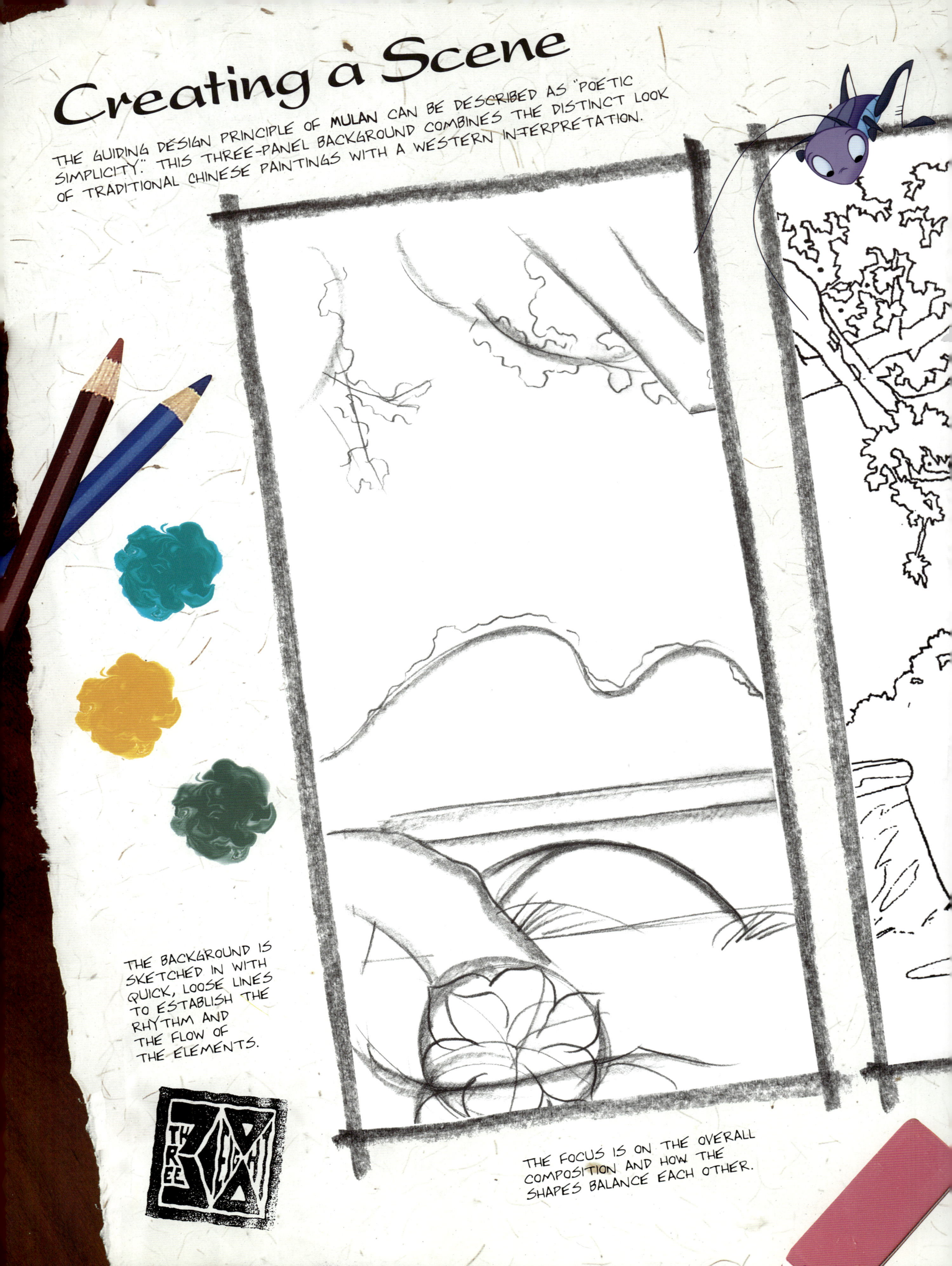

THE BACKGROUND IS SKETCHED IN WITH QUICK, LOOSE LINES TO ESTABLISH THE RHYTHM AND THE FLOW OF THE ELEMENTS.

THE FOCUS IS ON THE OVERALL COMPOSITION AND HOW THE SHAPES BALANCE EACH OTHER.

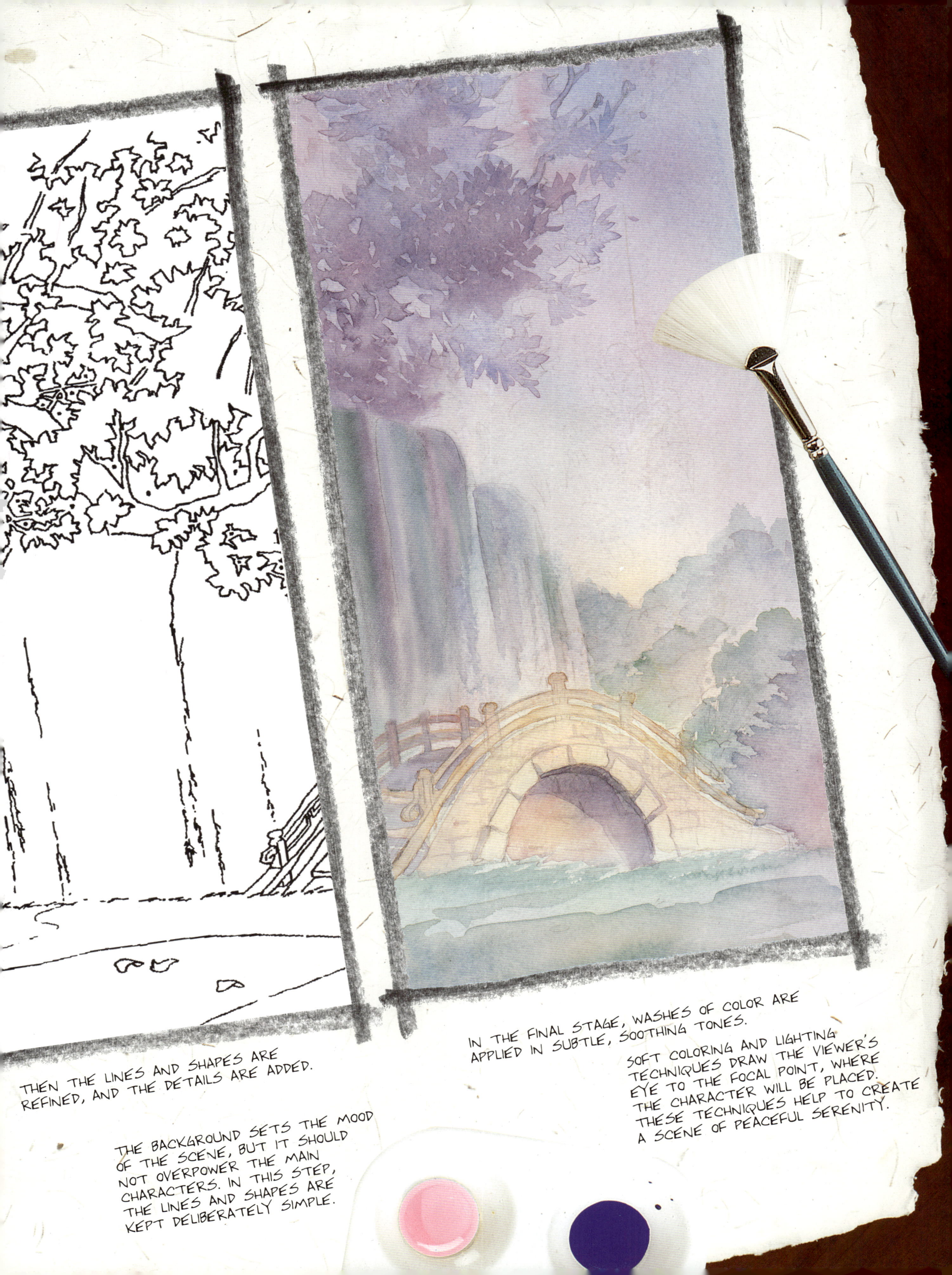

THEN THE LINES AND SHAPES ARE REFINED, AND THE DETAILS ARE ADDED.

THE BACKGROUND SETS THE MOOD OF THE SCENE, BUT IT SHOULD NOT OVERPOWER THE MAIN CHARACTERS. IN THIS STEP, THE LINES AND SHAPES ARE KEPT DELIBERATELY SIMPLE.

IN THE FINAL STAGE, WASHES OF COLOR ARE APPLIED IN SUBTLE, SOOTHING TONES.

SOFT COLORING AND LIGHTING TECHNIQUES DRAW THE VIEWER'S EYE TO THE FOCAL POINT, WHERE THE CHARACTER WILL BE PLACED. THESE TECHNIQUES HELP TO CREATE A SCENE OF PEACEFUL SERENITY.

Finale

NOW THAT YOU HAVE LEARNED ABOUT MULAN THROUGH THE EYES OF THE DISNEY ANIMATORS, YOU CAN DRAW THE FILM'S EXOTIC CAST OF CHARACTERS YOURSELF. TRY YOUR HAND AT RE-CREATING THE UNIQUE LOOK AND THE LYRICAL ATMOSPHERE OF THE STORY'S CHINESE SETTING. GOOD LUCK!

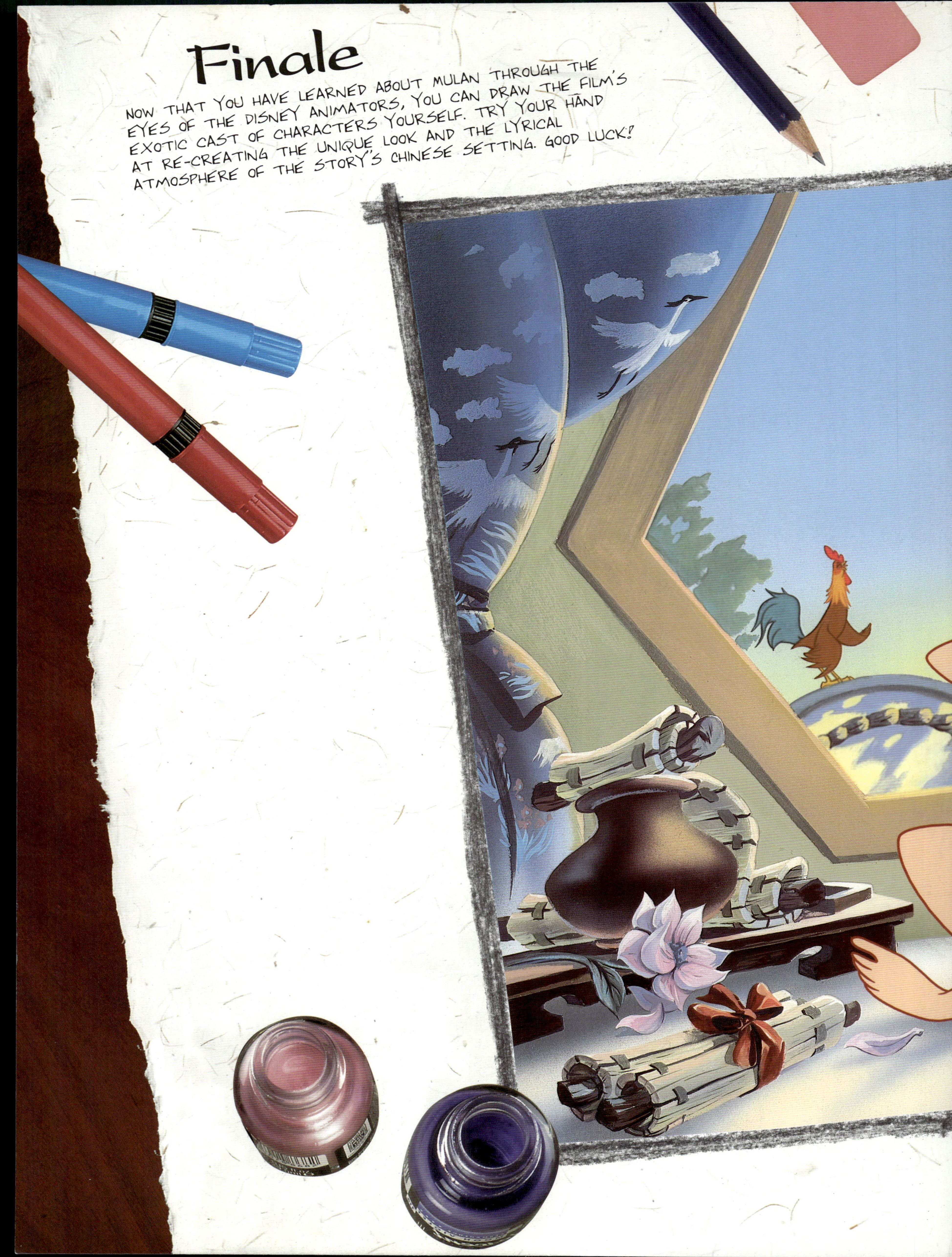